Living
Beyond
War

Living Beyond War

A Citizen's Guide

WINSLOW MYERS

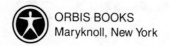

ORBIS BOOKS
Maryknoll, New York

Founded in 1970, Orbis Books endeavors to publish works that enlighten the mind, nourish the spirit, and challenge the conscience. The publishing arm of the Maryknoll Fathers and Brothers, Orbis seeks to explore the global dimensions of the Christian faith and mission, to invite dialogue with diverse cultures and religious traditions, and to serve the cause of reconciliation and peace. The books published reflect the views of their authors and do not represent the official position of the Maryknoll Society. To learn more about Maryknoll and Orbis Books, please visit our website at www.maryknollsociety.org.

Library of Congress Cataloging in Publication Data

Myers, Winslow.
  Living beyond war : a citizen's guide / Winslow Myers.
    p. cm.
  ISBN 978-1-57075-827-0 (pbk.)
  1. War and society. 2. Conflict management. 3. International relations. 4. War and society—United States. 5. Conflict management—United States. 6. United States—Foreign relations. I. Title.
  HM554.M94   2009
  303.6'9—dc22

                              2008043947

Contents

Foreword

Brian Swimme

Just imagine, at one time there was only hydrogen gas in the universe. So much has come forth. And each new emergence required a specific great work. Carbon atoms could not emerge until stars were assembled. Primitive life could not come forth until rocky planets were shaped. Symphonic music and mathematical physics could not be articulated until cities had been built. Thus we come to our own moment in cosmic history. A shining planet is about to burst forth into a blue-green flame of life and celebration. What is required for this birth is a new kind of human relationship, the contours of which are carefully laid out in this wise and practical book, *Living Beyond War: A Citizen's Guide*. As you read, you might quickly notice that you are growing in confidence concerning your life. For you will begin to realize, in a deep way, what life is asking of us. By reading this book you will come to know the decision that will put you at the most advanced wave of cosmological and terrestrial evolution. You will learn how to join with those who are pouring their lives into this work of bringing forth a beautiful world. You might even come to realize that this book is teaching you how to live the truth that the spiritual geniuses of history discovered. Nothing will bring greater joy than waking up each morning with the excitement of joining this creative project. And perhaps no other life will be as deeply praised by future humans. This work, whose side effect is to draw forth our noblest human qualities, will enable a new Earth Community to blossom forth, one as different from the twentieth-century Earth as a butterfly is from a cloud of hydrogen gas.

INTRODUCTION
A Dream Whose Time Has Come

Although the abolition of war has been the dream of man for centuries, every proposition to that end has been promptly discarded as impossible and fantastic. But that was before the science of the past decade made mass destruction a reality. The argument then was [only] along spiritual and moral lines, and lost. But now the tremendous evolution of nuclear and other potentials of destruction has suddenly taken the problem away from its primary consideration as a moral and spiritual question and brought it abreast of scientific realism. It is no longer an ethical question to be pondered solely by learned philosophers and ecclesiastics, but a hard-core one for the decision of the masses whose survival is the issue.
— Gen. Douglas MacArthur, 1961[1]

We each have an individual story, part unique and part universal: we are all born; we will all die. In between we all experience a measure of joy and sadness, anger and fear, hope and despair. We all seek survival in a chaotic and difficult world. If we are fortunate, the inevitable tests and trials of life teach us something that can be given back or passed on as proven wisdom: the possibility of a more meaningful connection with one another and an opportunity to be part of something greater than ourselves.[2]

Our unique stories nest within a larger story, the story of nations, religions, and ethnic groups that have often been at war. We absorb the drumbeat of violence and wonder why our world remains so alienated and brutal year after year, decade after decade. The United States slips out of the stalemate of the Korean War only to drift into another ambiguous war on Asian soil. We bring fifty years of Cold War to a nonviolent resolution only to find a new antagonism growing between the West and the Middle East. Genocide, which the world forswore after the liberation of the Nazi concentration camps in 1945, has been repeated in Cambodia, Bosnia, Rwanda, and elsewhere.

The prevailing model of geopolitical security, a relic of centuries of nation-states attempting to maintain their position in the global pecking order, continues to be the balance of separate and opposing political powers—with terrorism seeping in as an illusory shortcut to power for the powerless. The events unfolding as this was written are a "spheres of influence" case in point, disheartening yet not unexpected: Russia and the United States are once again at loggerheads. The small nation of Georgia, formerly part of the Soviet Union and directly adjacent to Russia, has sought membership in NATO. Russia is concerned not only about Georgia but also about American missile defense systems proposed for Eastern Europe. A Russian general even threatened a nuclear attack on Poland should these systems be deployed. It is hard not to be reminded of the United States' own visceral concern with the presence of a Soviet client-state ninety miles off the coast of Florida. Yet at the same time that Cold War tensions seem to be reviving, the United States deeply needs Russia's cooperation both in preventing Iran from acquiring nuclear weapons (the United States has insisted that the missile defense systems in Poland are intended only to defend against possible missiles from countries such as Iran) and in sequestering loose nuclear materials from terrorists.

The crisis in Georgia in August of 2008 is one more incident in the unfolding stream of "local" conflicts with planetary implications. Leaders of countries large and small, fearing most of all to be perceived as appeasers of the powers and interests that seem arrayed against them, often ratchet up the confrontational rhetoric as if they had no other choice. But now that a number of nations possess nuclear weapons, what looked in the past like reliable conceptions of power and toughness are trumped by the destructive power of the weapons themselves. A nuclear war would not be a manageable event, let alone a victory for anyone; it would be an unspeakably tragic mismanagement of the current security paradigm.

More than sixty years after the first detonation on Earth of a nuclear weapon, the human species has not yet come to terms with the presence of thousands of warheads around the globe. The issue still drives the most fateful policy decisions made by nations. One of the express reasons for the U.S. preemptive attack on Iraq, however misguided, was the possibility of finding nuclear or other weapons of mass destruction. National leaders assume they need to bring the power of these weapons to the negotiating table in order to be respected. Nuclear weapons have been a major theme of the bellicose rhetoric between Iran and the United States. Although the general level of anxiety about such weapons may be lower today than before the Cold War ended in the late 1980s, when millions poured into the streets of Western Europe to protest, the possibility of nuclear terror inhabits our nightmares. The presence of nuclear weapons has changed our planet, as they have changed war, forever.

The story of nations and cultures in violent conflict itself nests within an even larger story, the story of the Earth we all inhabit together. During the Cold War, people used to speculate how quickly humans would set aside their quarrels and unite if aliens invaded the Earth from space, or a large asteroid menaced the planet. Nuclear weapons, alongside our global environmental challenges, have the same capacity as an incoming asteroid to unite us in meeting a common challenge. As Pogo perceptively remarked, "We have met the enemy and he is us."[3]

Our delicate life-support system and our very existence as a species are threatened by an old way of thinking that rationalizes war, however distasteful, as a justifiable last resort. But war is a weapon of mass distraction. It drains away the energy and resources needed to stabilize the climate, feed the hungry, and get our economic house in order. War thinking, "us-and-them" thinking, with its assumption of separation and alienation, keeps us from seeing and acting on our common fate. We still have not grasped the extent of our planetary interdependence. To put Pogo's wisdom in positive terms: to survive, our species needs to cooperate on a whole new level.

IMPRACTICAL, NAÏVE, AND UTOPIAN?

Many assume that the possibility that the people on this small planet could ever move beyond war is hopelessly idealistic and naïve. Or is it?

Humans have slowly learned the impracticality of using violence in day-to-day social interactions. Instead, we have evolved cultural rituals that allow our ordinary life to be nonviolent for the most part. This understanding has spread to the political relations of large regions, such as the peaceful associations among the fifty United States or the nations of the European Union. For hundreds of years the countries of Europe were a constant battleground. Today, they enjoy open borders, a common currency, and the negotiated resolution of disputes.

This hopeful direction in world affairs suggests that it is not naïve to think that we could leave the institution of war behind. What *is* naïve is to believe that the world will become safer as more nations try to obtain genocidal weapons and as stronger nations reserve the right to invade weaker ones in order to prevent further proliferation. Much of humanity already recognizes this naiveté. Of the approximately 194 nations on the planet, only nine possess nuclear weapons. Four attained but renounced them, and seventeen tried to make them but gave up. There are 189 countries, including five that have nuclear weapons, who are signatories to the Nuclear Non-Proliferation Treaty. That so many countries have agreed to renounce such weapons indicates that most of us already realize that war, especially nuclear war, has become a no-win option. At the same time, though treaties have clearly slowed proliferation, the number of countries with nuclear weapons continues to increase. The list as of 2008 includes China, Russia, the United States, Israel, France, Britain, India, Pakistan, and North Korea.

Because any minor point of tension in the balance of powers among all nations could potentially lead to war, and any such war could escalate into nuclear war, moving beyond war, far from being utopian, is a realistic necessity, in the same way that anticipating the effects of global climate change is a realistic necessity. When a practical military man like Gen. MacArthur entertains the notion of abolishing war, it seems less like saintly idealism and more like a goal worthy of sober consideration. And something else is happening to turn possibility into probability.

A GRASSROOTS UPWELLING

While nightly news programs continue to carry reports of wars large and small, a remarkable mass movement is occurring planetwide that has received insufficient recognition in the mainstream press. Over a million grassroots nongovernmental organizations have sprung up around the globe with a shared core of values that include nonviolence, human rights, gender equality, economic justice, and sustainability. Such groups feed our innate desire for connection and meaningful action in the midst of impersonal social forces that seem too powerful to change.

Clayton Thomas-Muller speaks to a community gathering of the Cree nation about waste sites on their native land in Northern Alberta, toxic lakes so big you can see them from outer space. Shi Lihong, founder of Wild China Films, makes documentaries with her husband on migrants displaced by construction of large dams. Rosalina Tuyuc Velásquez, a member of the Maya-Kaqchikel people, fights for full accountability for tens of thousands of people killed by death squads in Guatemala. Rodrigo Baggio retrieves discarded computers from New York, London, and Toronto and installs them in the favelas of Brazil, where he and his staff teach computer skills to poor children. Biologist Janine Benyus speaks to twelve hundred executives at a business forum in Queensland about biologically inspired industrial development . . . Silas Kpanan'Ayoung Siakor, who exposed links between the genocidal policies of former president Charles Taylor and illegal logging in Liberia, now creates certified, sustainable timber policies.[4]

Paul Hawken defines this upsurge of citizen involvement as the largest mass movement in the history of the world.[5] Hawken is not alone in his appreciation of this emerging global phenomenon. In *Beyond Bullets and Bombs*, Judith Kurliansky reports on many initiatives being taken by Israelis and Palestinians to bring each other into a positive relationship, including a number of peace camps that allow young people from both sides to overcome their alienation and to experience connection.[6] Even networking Web sites like Facebook are being used as instruments of peacemaking. An organization called Global Mindshift is encouraging international conversation on topics of planetwide interest, conducted entirely in virtual reality.[7] With a few clicks of a mouse, we can exchange ideas and concerns with someone in Tibet, Iceland, the Congo. People from 125 countries are participating. These citizen-initiated and citizen-led initiatives complement state-sponsored peace and reconciliation processes, such as the work of Senator Mitchell in Northern Ireland or of Nelson Mandela and Desmond Tutu in South Africa.

Whether such initiatives begin with governments or their citizens, they address crises that are interwoven. Many would assert that there are other issues at least as urgent as the prevention of war, such as limiting climate change and population growth, preventing AIDS and managing its devastating effects, sustaining the global supply of food or water, helping the African continent find its footing in the world economy, or preventing the collapse of world fisheries. A successful resolution of any of these challenges is linked with ending war in one broad sense: war causes destruction and chaos that make sustainable social development far more difficult, and, in the case of nuclear war, impossible.

The presumption that war will always be with us continues to pervade the thinking of leaders and citizens alike. The emerging paradigm represented by the initiatives burgeoning around the globe remains fragile. But as this mass movement of citizen involvement continues to grow, a tipping-point may arrive.[8] New values will seep into and finally become mainstream thinking. When this happens, established institutions with undeserved reputations for ineffectiveness, first among them the United Nations, will receive new impetus for missions that have been indispensable all along. The upsurge of renewal from below will integrate with a new international consensus from above.

A GUIDEBOOK FOR ENDING WAR

While our species is all too familiar with the power to degrade or even destroy life on a mass scale, we still have much to learn about the even greater power to sustain life that is potential within us all. The purpose of this book is to help unleash that power. The book is intended to supplement the work of an organization called Beyond War,[9] one of the millions of NGOs working at the grassroots level to introduce a new way of thinking and acting. Beyond War's mission is educational: to help people explore, model, and promote the means for humanity to live without war. This book complements the organization's resources in other media, such as the Beyond War Web site, or DVDs that enable presentations and conversations in homes, businesses, churches, temples, and mosques. It is intended to help people converse with and listen patiently to others who still believe that war is a good idea, or at worst a necessary evil.

The way of thinking presented here, though partially rooted in the world's major wisdom traditions, is also based on practical reasons for ending war. This book is emphatically not just for people who think of themselves as liberals or progressives, but also for those whose convictions may be deeply conservative. It will make sense not only to Lutherans in Nebraska and Unitarians in New Jersey, but also to Muslims in Isfahan, Hindus in New Delhi, Jews in Israel, Buddhists in Osaka, atheists in Beijing, and agnostics in Bordeaux.

Moving beyond war will require an immense systemic shift in values, a shift that depends on new agreements on the deep level of principle. The particular examples chosen to make the case, such as the Iraq war or the tensions in Georgia, may gradually become dated as the headlines are taken over by new crises, but the principles themselves will not. This book is based upon self-evident truths that are applicable across diverse cultures, principles that are relevant not just to events in Iraq or Palestine or the Congo, but also to any future conflict. However intractable the dispute, it will be truly resolved only by some variation of the nonviolent processes outlined here.

Although building a world beyond war calls on many disciplines, from biology and anthropology to international law and diplomacy, this book is designed for ordinary citizens rather than for experts and specialists. Every assertion can be verified by individual experience and put into practice immediately without waiting for anyone or anything else to change—except ourselves. By the end, the reader not only will realize that we are each individually essential to ending war but also will understand a practical process for getting from the "here" of a world where war is still acceptable to the "there" of a world beyond war. Three principles will guide us from here to there.

THREE GUIDING PRINCIPLES

War Is Obsolete

The use of the word "obsolete" is deliberate. Webster's defines "obsolete" as outmoded, no longer current, regarded as out-of-date whether in use or not—with the implication that there is something better. The fundamental reason that war is obsolete is the pervasive presence of nuclear weapons on the planet. Even a limited nuclear war would be suicidal for the participants and could even be "omnicidal" to the life systems of the Earth. War is obsolete, though, of course, it is still far from extinct.

Chapter 1 makes the case for the dysfunctionality of all war. Chapter 2 makes the case that nuclear war is the inevitable outgrowth of conventional war unless we change the way we think and act. On both levels, conventional and nuclear, war has become obsolete. It only puts further from our reach the security we all want. Chapter 3 explores the root cause of war: our ingrained assumption that we are separate and that others are different.

We Are One on This Planet

"We are one" is a shorthand way of stating a fundamental aspect of reality that has always been with us but is now more demonstrable than at any time in history. Ever since we first saw images of the whole Earth from space, our understanding of our interdependence as a species has deepened. We have experienced our vulnerable interrelationship in breathtaking images of the curve of our sea-blue globe with its luminous coating of air. There is only one atmosphere, not separate Judeo-Christian, Buddhist, and Islamic atmospheres. "Spaceship Earth" is reality, not just an attractive metaphor. We are all—conservative and progressive, Arab and Jew, Muslim and Sikh—equally threatened by the possibility of nuclear war, just as we are equally threatened by global environmental degradation.

But we rarely act this way in our daily interactions, let alone our international ones. Instead, we continue to assume that our self-interest and self-preservation are not intimately connected to everyone else's. We suffer from a deficit of the ethical imagination through which we could perceive and act on our connection with one another and all life. An open-minded look at the reality of our species-wide interdependence is laid out in chapters 4 and 5.

The Means Are the Ends in the Making

A third principle that will help to guide us beyond war derives inevitably from the first and second. "The means are the ends in the making" is the life-affirming opposite of "The ends justify the means." The path we as individuals and nations choose to follow determines where we will end up. If war doesn't work as a way to resolve conflict, and if all six billion humans share a common ecological destiny, then we can no longer use violent means to arrive at peaceful ends.

This book builds a case for the self-evident, life-or-death practicality of these three principles—and their implications for each of us personally. These personal implications are unavoidable. We cannot be credible advocates for a world beyond war unless we have decided to live beyond war in our daily lives. Three practices allow us to do this.

THREE CORE PRACTICES

In most discussions about war and violence, the talk settles upon "them"—the terrorists, the present administration, the other political party, the military-industrial-media complex, the congenitally violent—innumerable vague "others." Behind this talk of "them" are assumptions that "I" am helpless, that I cannot change until "they" change, and "they" aren't going to change. We rarely focus on the "me," the person over whom we have most control, the self through whom I can transform my own role in perpetuating ill will and war. The antidotes for this preoccupation with "them" are three simple but profound "I" statements that form the core personal practices of Beyond War.

- I will resolve conflict. I will not use violence.
- I will maintain an attitude of goodwill. I will not preoccupy myself with an enemy.
- I will work together with others to build a world beyond war.

Chapter 6 explores these core practices in depth.

Chapter 7 applies the guiding principles to the international scene, suggesting some of the alternatives to war that people and nations, without unilaterally disarming themselves, have already pursued with effective results.

DECISION AND ACTION

The last four chapters of the book examine the process of individual and social change. Chapter 8 describes surprising discoveries about the way change moves through societies, and outlines educational actions that citizens must undertake in order to build widespread agreement about the truth and utility of the guiding principles and core practices.

The overall structure of the book is a movement from relevant knowledge to decision and to action. Chapter 9, therefore, emphasizes the need for a personal decision to give up war. Chapter 10 describes the invaluable role of dialogue and listening once we have made that decision. A final chapter affirms our species' capacity for positive change.

LIVE THE QUESTIONS

Visionary leaders such Mahatma Gandhi and Martin Luther King demonstrated the power that comes from living in accordance with a strong set of principles. Can I, like them, learn to narrow the gap between my ideals and the way I actually live day by day? Is it possible to transform my feelings of anger, sadness, and frustration into something more constructive? What happens when I abandon war as an option? What changes in attitude within my family and among my circle of friends make it possible for me to abandon war? What would we need to do together to make it safe for our nation to seek alternatives to war? Can the world move beyond war if I myself remain uninvolved?

"Live the questions," suggested the poet Rainer Maria Rilke.[10] While most people reading this book may already have thought deeply about the issues it raises, it is helpful to get together with a group of people and have a conversation about whether the principles and practices laid out here adequately address the reality of contemporary planetary conditions. Two of the best ways to engage with the book are first, to be skeptical and to try to critique its major points with the strongest possible counterarguments, and second, to try out its ideas in order to see if they work in our own lives. Only then can we come to a place where we experience an autonomous sense of our own convictions. Therefore, a set of questions designed to stimulate dialogue is provided at the end of each chapter. The appendixes include documents from other writers that confirm and enrich the overall case—a case that is intended to be concise, credible, and authoritative.

AMERICAN LEADERSHIP

While this book may be translated into many languages, it has been written by Americans and is addressed first to Americans. Citizens of the United States are privileged to enjoy resources that invite us to take the lead in building a new way of thinking about conflict resolution and war. With the privileges of freedom, and a vastly greater prosperity than most of the world, comes responsibility. The liberties guaranteed by the U.S. Constitution provide a fertile environment for moving the world beyond war. There is no official religion or ideology in our country. Instead, our civic culture works through "the civil public square,"[11] where citizens are free to initiate dialogue in the open marketplace of ideas.

The true strength of our nation comes not from the might of our arms or the scale or our wealth, but from the enduring power of our ideals: democracy, liberty, opportunity, and unyielding hope.

—Barack Obama, November 4, 2008

The United States is a young country, a work in progress. We have not always lived up to the ideal of our founding principle, "all men are created equal." The application of that principle was at first limited to white, property-owning males. Later, its implication expanded sufficiently to free African Americans from slavery and, still later, to give women the vote. The dialogue about the full implications of our principles is far from finished. Nevertheless, the United States remains a beacon of hope because people throughout the world sense the commitment of its citizens to equality, transparency, and the rule of law.

The two-hundred-year process of ending slavery in the United States and worldwide is a good example of the process of social change for which this book advocates. The economies of many nations were deeply dependent on trade in human beings, just as the business of war and arms sales is deeply embedded in the U.S. and world economy today. At the beginning of the eighteenth century, the abandonment of slavery seemed inconceivable. The process began with a few individuals realizing that the institution was at cross-purposes with emerging notions of equal rights.

Those early abolitionists made lifelong commitments to pursue change, and because they did, what seemed impossible at the outset finally happened. Agreement slowly grew that slavery was a fundamental violation of human dignity, and eventually abolition followed. It is true that if we accept a wider definition of slavery that includes gross worker exploitation or child prostitution, the work of ending slavery is not over.[12] But no one would question the underlying ethical principles that energize that ongoing process. Slavery has been consigned to the dustbin of history. The time has come to do the same with war.

Moving beyond war does not necessitate or imply one-world government. It does mean that individual nations learn to abide by international laws that are applied fully and equally to all—the replacement of the law of force with the force of law. We know this level of agreement is already possible when the stakes are high enough. We saw this when the ozone layer was threatened and a worldwide ban on the use of chlorofluorocarbons was rapidly put in place. The United States, with the most robust military in the world, is strong enough to help lead the transition to a world beyond war without compromising its own security. Making the transition successfully will vastly increase that security.

LIVING BEYOND WAR TODAY

Paul Hawken's upsurge of grassroots experiments includes many successful models from around the world of living beyond war. One of them is in a surprising place, a village thirty miles west of Jerusalem, Neve Shalom/Wahat al Salaam, which means "oasis of peace" in Hebrew and Arabic. Here, Jews and Muslims have been living, working, and raising their children together since 1978. It is home to over fifty families, half Jewish-Israeli and half Muslim-Israeli, and three hundred families are on a waiting list. Residents make a living by operating a bilingual, bicultural school so good that once-hostile people in the surrounding areas now send their children to be educated there. Children grow up celebrating each other's holidays and traditions. They learn to respect one another while being true to themselves. It has not been easy, but the community is a living example in a very conflicted part of the world that what seems impossible is not only possible but also practical.

While the subject of ensuring the continuation of life on our planet is about as serious as can be, it need not be depressing or hopeless. The change of thinking advocated by this book includes moving beyond anger and outrage to a place where laughter and genuine optimism are possible. Because the means are the ends in the making, the voyage itself is the destination. The need to move beyond war is an urgent wake-up call, but it is also an opportunity to make relationships with people, which is one of the deepest human pleasures and rewards. Although building a world beyond war will require hard work, it is one of the most richly fulfilling activities imaginable. In a dark time, by doing this work, we can feel ourselves drawn into a circle of light. It is, in the words of the Peace Corps motto, "the toughest job you'll ever love."

You never change things by fighting existing reality . . . To change something, build a new model that makes the existing models obsolete.

—Buckminster Fuller[13]

QUESTIONS FOR DIALOGUE

1. Was there a point in your life when you began to question whether war might not be the best option to resolve conflict? Who were some of the people, or what were some of the experiences or readings, that suggested other options?

2. How would you define the uniqueness of the current moment in history?

NOTES

1. Gen. Douglas MacArthur, address to the Philippines Congress, 1961.

2. See Joseph Campbell, *The Hero with a Thousand Faces*, 3rd ed. (Novato, CA: New World Library, 2008).

3. Pogo, a wise possum, was a twentieth-century cartoon character drawn by Walt Kelly.

4. Paul Hawken, "To Remake the World," *Orion Magazine* (May/June 2007): 3.

5. Paul Hawken, *Blessed Unrest* (New York: Penguin, 2007).

6. Judy Kuriansky, *Beyond Bullets and Bombs: Grassroots Peacebuilding between Israelis and Palestinians* (Westport, CT: Praeger, 2008).

7. http://www.global-mindshift.org.

8. See Malcolm Gladwell, *The Tipping Point* (Boston: Back Bay Books, 2002).

9. Beyond War is a 501(c)(3) nonprofit foundation. See www.beyondwar.org for contact information. See also Acknowledgments, p. 178.

10. Rainer Maria Rilke, *Letters to a Young Poet* (New York: W. W. Norton, 1993).

11. Os Guinness, *The American Hour: A Time of Reckoning and the Once and Future Role of Faith* (New York: Free Press, 1993), 20.

12. Matt Renner, "Slavery Today: A Clear and Present Danger," http://www.truthout.org/article/slavery-today-a-clear-and-present-danger.

13. Buckminster Fuller, 1895-1983, philosopher, inventor, futurist. See http://bfi.org/change.

PART ONE

WAR IS OBSOLETE

Man will put an end to war, or war will put an end to man.
—John F. Kennedy, 1961

1

War Doesn't Work

War is obviously far from *extinct*—but war has become *obsolete*—for four overarching reasons:

- War doesn't solve the very problems that often tempt us to choose it either as a preventive option or a last resort.
- The costs of war and the preparation for war have become unacceptably high.
- The destructiveness of modern weapons means that, as President Kennedy asserted over a half century ago, either we will end war or war will end us.
- There are far better alternatives.[1]

WAR IS DYSFUNCTIONAL

War is an instrument entirely inefficient toward redressing wrong: and multiplies, instead of indemnifying losses.
—Thomas Jefferson, 1810[2]

 During the Cold War between the Soviet Union and the United States, it became clear to citizens and policy makers alike that the two superpowers could conceivably get into a small war or proxy war somewhere on the planet that could escalate into a world-scale, even life-extinguishing, catastrophe. Today, the pervasive assumption is that such an all-out war is considerably less likely. Chapter 2 will explore this fatal aspect of war and demonstrate that the conditions for such a catastrophe are more present than ever. They can be found in the lethal combination of proliferation, possible misinterpretation in command-and-control systems, and the potentiality of small wars to escalate into nuclear confrontations. All war has the potential to become nuclear war.

But even if it does not, war on any level has become so destructive that it is dysfunctional. It does not yield the results for which we hope when we choose the war option. Iraq as of 2008 is a case in point, a perfect storm of dysfunctionality.

In time, the war in Iraq, including the conflicts among various religious, political, and tribal factions within the country, will have wound down. By then Iraq may no longer even exist as a discrete nation or may have taken a political form that we would not even recognize today—we hope, of course, an autonomous, stable national identity that will benefit all the Iraqi people, Shia, Sunni, Kurdish, and others, no matter what their ethnic, religious, or tribal affiliation. By what measure will the United States determine what constitutes success in our campaign there? What is best for the United States alone, or what is truly best for all Iraqis? Were the benefits of an extended occupation worth the high cost of alienation, blood, and treasure paid by Iraqis and Americans and others? Worth the millions of Iraqis turned into refugees? Have we, as the Roman historian Tacitus wrote, "made a desolation and called it peace"? Or were there other more creative and effective alternatives for dealing with terrorism and fostering democratic institutions in the region?

Some argue that the war we have waged in Afghanistan is qualitatively different from the U.S. campaign in Iraq, because the extremists who brought down the twin towers received their training in its remote mountains. But, again, the larger question becomes whether the United States couldn't have thought more outside the war box. One alternative is suggested by Greg Mortenson's bestseller *Three Cups of Tea,* his account of building schools in northwestern Pakistan and Afghanistan.[3] The most significant response to terrorism may not be military at all; it may lie in the education of Afghan women, who will bring up their children to be less susceptible to extremism. Greg and his schools have been left alone by the Taliban because the villages trust the disinterest-edness of Greg's motives. By contrast, the history of the region is one of many outside forces, including the British and the Soviets, failing to subdue the tribal areas of Afghanistan to their own ends. Adding to the policy confusion is the contrast between Iraq and Afghanistan, the former containing a sea of oil, which the West covets, and the latter a sea of poppies, which fuels the worldwide trade in heroin.

At the same time, in spite of the unforgettable lesson of the Jewish holocaust, we know that humans are still capable of descent into genocide, as we have seen in Cambodia, Bosnia, Rwanda, Darfur, and even, on a smaller but no less lethal scale, on the streets of Baghdad. Depending on how efficiently the community of nations can cooperate to head off such disasters, timely initia-tives to prevent genocide need not be thought of as war in the traditional sense of aggression to gain unilateral advantage. There is a significant difference between wars undertaken to annihilate an enemy and police actions designed to deescalate conflict and protect noncombatants. But even such police actions have often been ineffective or come too late, which suggests that the world as a whole has serious work to do in order to get to the point where genocide and other forms of mass violence become incon-ceivable.

If we are tempted to "distance" genocide into something only other, less socially stable countries descend into, it is essential to remind ourselves that the superpowers possess thousands of potentially genocidal weapons. One of the express motivations for the invasion of Iraq was to deny its leaders any possibility of building such weapons themselves. While not all conventional wars in the twenty-first century are associated with nuclear weap-ons, the global war on terrorism certainly is. In both the war with Iraq and the ongoing tensions with Iran, the United States has been especially concerned that nuclear weapons, if acquired by these countries or others, could fall into the hands of governmen-tal or extragovernmental extremists.

THE "WAR ON TERROR"

War does not, and cannot, defeat terrorism, even nuclear terrorism. In fact, war is an ineffective and dangerous response to terrorism. War has traditionally been waged against identifiable adversaries and their infrastructure within specific boundaries. Terrorism, by contrast, is not a place or a country. When terrorists hide among an indigenous populace, it is counterproductive if not impossible to bomb them. There is no finite number of terrorists, and, because they often operate independently, they are not always under the control of a central authority. That makes it difficult for them to negotiate in the way discrete countries traditionally negotiate. Terrorism itself is a strategy, a tactic. It is impossible to win a war against a strategy in the way nations have historically won wars against nations. A 2008 study by the conservative think tank Rand Corporation found that 43 percent of past insurgencies and terrorist movements dissolved by inclusion into political processes, 40 percent were contained by effective police and intelligence work, and only 7 percent were overcome by conventional military initiatives.[4]

The respected international mediator John Paul Lederach has asserted that going to war to defeat terrorism is like hitting a mature dandelion with a golf club . . . It only creates another generation of terrorists.[5] We saw the truth of this in Iraq, where al-Qaeda was not initially present, but certainly became present later, whether as an offshoot of Osama bin Laden's original movement or as an autonomous franchise, in response to what was perceived as a neocolonial occupation by a foreign power.

In his book *Dying to Win,* Professor Robert Pape of the University of Chicago examines in depth the phenomenon of suicide bombing.[6] His research reveals that though religious conviction or revenge may play a role, suicide bombings always include the primary motivation of trying to push out foreign occupiers.[7] According to Pape, a number of stereotypes about terrorism turn out to be less than accurate, such as that terrorists are poor or uneducated, or that suicidal terrorism is part of a broad-based Islamic strategy to conquer the world.

Much as we are tempted to preserve a unique level of outrage for the nineteen men (fifteen from Saudi Arabia, one from Egypt, two from the United Arab Emirates, and one from Lebanon) who perpetrated the horrors of September 11, 2001, it may turn out to be more useful in the long run to have remained with a definition of such people as violent criminals. Adherence to an international legal system could limit the activities of these criminals more effectively than old-style national war making. It is far more efficient for the community of nations to intensify the cooperation of police around the world and to bring terrorists before existing systems of justice. And all countries have a common interest in helping one another account for every ounce of nuclear-grade material globally, guarding it securely against theft or black-market sale.

Going to war and dropping bombs that kill innocent people who do not initially condone deeds of terrorism only perpetuate and enlarge a cycle of violence. When Timothy McVeigh bombed the Federal Courthouse in Oklahoma City, no one suggested we should bomb his hometown. Instead, our criminal justice system was set in motion, identified him, and brought him to justice.

THE MANY COSTS OF WAR

A second reason war is obsolete is its unacceptably high cost. War has so many costs that it is difficult to keep them all in mind at once.

Death

War, not unlike terrorism, is about killing, hurting, and breaking the spirit of adversaries. Even for militaries that pride themselves on using "smart" bombs, most deaths in war continue to be non-combatant, as they were in World War I, when more than ten million civilians were killed. Civilian deaths in the Soviet Union during World War II numbered twice the military deaths. In the civil war in the Democratic Republic of Congo, 5.4 million people have died,[8] though many in the West have never even heard of this conflict, the worst since World War II. Exact statistics for civilian deaths in the Iraq war are hard to come by, but as of 2008, conservative estimates suggest that roughly 100,000 noncombatants had been killed in Iraq as a direct or indirect result of the U.S. invasion. The United Nations estimates that half a million Iraqi children age five or under died in the decade after the first Gulf War, most from water-borne diseases.

Permanent Physical or Psychological Injury

Soldiers and civilians on all sides, if they are not killed outright, often emerge from war with physical or psychological injuries that limit them for the rest of their lives and can affect families and children into further generations. The widespread use of Agent Orange to defoliate the jungles of Vietnam resulted in thousands of birth defects in both the children of Vietnamese civilians and of American veterans. In the conflicts in Darfur and the Congo, the rape of women and young girls as an instrument of war has been epidemic.[9] Many if not most U.S. soldiers who have endured active combat in Iraq suffer from serious stress reactions as a result of what they saw or did. Others return disfigured, missing limbs, or brain damaged to the extent of requiring lifetime care. CBS News reported that during 2005 at least 120 American veterans of all wars killed themselves *per week,* a rate twice that of Americans as a whole.[10] Wars keep on killing and maiming long after active conflict has ended. Mines sown during the Vietnam War and many other wars continue to threaten civilians decades later.

Destruction of Social and Physical Infrastructure

Another tremendous cost of war is the fraying of the fabric that makes a peaceful and civil society possible. Many of the hundreds of thousands of people who have fled Iraq since the beginning of the second Gulf War were doctors, teachers, and engineers who were essential to the social cohesion of the country. Hospitals, schools, and water systems were destroyed, and sources of energy and electric power were disrupted, which complicates reconstruction efforts.

Torture and the Loss of Rights

A further cost of war is the subtle erosion or outright loss of the hard-won rights guaranteed by governments. Some constitutional rights were suspended during the American Civil War. Thousands of Japanese Americans were unfairly interred in camps during World War II. After September 11, 2001, the temptation became strong to cross the murky borderline beyond which governments condone the torture of adversaries. Gradually Americans have found themselves complicit in such abhorrent acts as waterboarding, for which the allies sentenced enemy combatants in World War II to years of hard labor.[11]

The Cycle of Violence

Each war, rather than truly resolving whatever conflict began it, provides justification for the losers to lick their wounds, continue to stereotype the winners as evil and unjust, and wait for the day when they can take their revenge. Perhaps the most important twentieth-century example is the way the seeds of Nazism were sown by the humiliation suffered by the defeated Germans after World War I. Years after the end of the Cold War, Russia's sense that it suffered a diminishment of prestige and power as the result of the breakup of the Soviet empire is part of what motivates its nervous belligerence today. In Afghanistan as in Iraq, adversaries are distributed within the civilian population, making a high number of noncombatant casualties inevitable and strengthening the motivation to retaliate in kind. Hard feelings create a vicious circle that can continue for generations.

In war, leaders and followers demonize opponents, forgetting that they are enmeshed in a historical cycle that, in the minds of aggrieved parties, could be hundreds of years old. Too often this has been the case in the relations between the Middle East and the West, where memories persist not just of the CIA's manipulation of politics in Iran in the 1950s or colonial attempts to gain advantage by the Western powers during and after World War I, but all the way back to medieval crusades. The separate narratives of grievance and contested ownership asserted by Israelis and Palestinians go back still further, to biblical times.

Unintended Consequences

Would President Nixon have bombed Cambodia had he known that the resulting disintegration of the country would lead to the rise of the Khmer Rouge and the genocidal deaths of two million people? Would the American CIA have armed the mujahideen in Afghanistan[12] if they had known that it would help spur the Soviets to invade, and eventually result in the rise of the Taliban and their protection of Osama Bin Laden? Would the United States have invaded Iraq if we had known it would begin a civil war between Shia and Sunni that resulted in the disintegration of the country, the destabilization of the region, and the near ruin of the reputation of the United States worldwide?

The Spread of Arms

The *New York Times* reported in November 2006 that the Bush administration and American military contractors doubled international arms sales from $10.6 billion to $21 billion from September 2005 to September 2006. Lawrence Korb, assistant defense secretary under President Reagan, told the *Boston Globe* in 1996, "The brakes are off the system . . . There is no coherent policy on the transfer of arms. It has become a money game; an absurd spiral into which we export arms only to have to develop more sophisticated ones to counter those spread all over the world . . ."[13] In 2006 the United States accounted for 52 percent of all arms sales in the world.[14]

Corruption and Profiteering

The chaos of war encourages lawless arrangements that operate outside the checks and balances of working governments and allow underground markets that enrich the few to the detriment of the common interest. Billions of dollars of U.S. taxpayer money has poured into Iraq with no clear record of where it went or what it paid for, with the amounts dwarfing the U.N. oil-for-food scandal that was one source of international frustration with both Saddam Hussein and the United Nations itself.[15]

Mercenaries

An additional pernicious cost of war has resurfaced in the modern world in the form of the private armies such as the huge Blackwater firm employed by the United States to protect diplomatic and business officials or to help gather intelligence.[16] Such mercenaries raise the specter of military power available to the highest bidder and legally unaccountable to elected civilian officials.

Dollar Costs

In fiscal year 2008, the United States plans to spend more on its military forces—623 billion dollars—than all the rest of the nations of the world—*combined*.[17] By the Pentagon's own count, the United States has over 760 bases in 39 countries around the world,[18] and these are only the nonclassified bases. Military budgets are self-perpetuating systems with a momentum that is not necessarily guided by a grounded sense of security requirements. National leaders maintain their electability by playing upon fears that we are falling behind other nations militarily. In 1958, Senator John F. Kennedy received significant political mileage out of his concept of a "missile gap," when the truth was that the Soviet military was far behind the United States in both the quantity and technological quality of its hardware. Legislators want large military projects to be built in their districts, ensuring local prosperity and their own re-election. Weapons manufacturers want new contracts in order to keep their stockholders content. In 2007, 43 cents of every American tax dollar went to the military.[19] Nobel Prize–winning economist Paul Stiglitz estimates that the Iraq war could end up costing over three *trillion* dollars,[20] creating a mountain of debt that will inevitably impact the economic health of our children and grandchildren. Waging war often involves a lethal assault not only on our adversaries but also on our economic self-interest.

Costs in Lost Opportunities

Too many scientists who could be researching new sources of clean energy or discovering life-saving vaccines are focused instead on thinking up new and more efficient ways to annihilate other human beings. Military budgets siphon off resources that might have been used to repair levees in New Orleans or provide universal health care. As of this writing, forty-seven million Americans were without health insurance.[21] Many essentials of a vibrant society, including education, transportation, and social services, have suffered from our skewed budgetary emphasis on military power. In terms of increasing our social capital, weapons are a poor investment compared to schools, hospitals, or energy-saving systems of transport.

Shortly after 9/11, the writer John Robbins put the costs of war in lost opportunities in a context that gives a poignant human meaning to the mind-numbing statistics:

Approximately 3,000 people perished in the September 11 attacks. Our nation still reels from such despicable brutality. But those who died from the attacks on that tragic day were not alone. On September 11th, 35,000 children worldwide died of hunger. A similar number of children died on September 12, and again on the 13th, and on every single day since . . .

To advance human security and control terrorism, we must not find only the brutality of the September 11th attacks to be totally intolerable. We must also find intolerable that one billion people worldwide survive on $1 a day, that more than one billion people lack access to safe drinking water, and that three billion people have inadequate access to sanitation. We have not hesitated to build an international coalition and to spend hundreds of millions of dollars to defeat those who launched the attacks on September 11th. What if we were equally as dedicated to building an international coalition to eradicate hunger, to provide clean water, to curb infectious disease, to provide adequate jobs, to combat illiteracy, and to end homelessness?

This goal is too costly, many say. But that is not true.

The cost of our initial military response in Afghanistan will top $100 billion beyond our already enormous annual defense budget of $342 billion. What could we accomplish if we spent even a small fraction of that on programs to alleviate human suffering? In 1998, the United Nations Development Program estimated that it would cost an additional $9 billion (above current expenditures) to provide clean water for everyone on Earth. It would cost an additional $12 billion, they said, to cover reproductive health services for all women worldwide. Another $13 billion would be enough not only to give every person on Earth enough food to eat but also basic health care. An additional $6 billion would provide basic education for all. These are large numbers, but combined they add up to $40 billion—only one fifth as much as the $200 billion the U.S. government agreed in October 2001 to pay Lockheed to build the new F-35 Joint Strike Fighter (JSF) jets.[22]

It is striking that Americans were easily able to write a check to themselves for 700 billion dollars intended to continue the prosperity of those of us who already enjoy clean water, adequate food, and decent medical care—an amount seventeen and a half times larger than what Robbins asserts would be sufficient to heal some of the world's most painful sore spots.

An entrepreneurial creativity that addresses all our many challenges of sustainability will be crucial to sustaining peace itself. Environmental stresses move closer to irreversibility. How is this particularly relevant to the abolition of war? It is becoming clearer with each passing year that one cause of potential future wars, as John Robbins implies, could be conflicts over adequate sources of clean water or arable land.[23] The U.S. military spends billions to protect existing fossil-fuel energy sources, billions that might be better invested directly in developing new alternative sources.

In all their variety, the costs of war are so high that they cry out for us to try other ways of resolving conflict. But the biggest potential cost of war, worthy of a separate chapter, is contained in the omnicidal power of modern weapons of mass destruction.

QUESTIONS FOR DIALOGUE

1. Most of us believe war is a necessary evil. What benefits do we derive from this belief?

2. What benefits would we derive from shifting to a belief that war doesn't work?
3. What is the evidence supporting each of these beliefs?
4. Is war a viable model for ending terrorism? Why or why not? Is it possible for nations to "stamp out" terrorism by overwhelming military force alone?
5. What would constitute "victory" in the "war on terror"? What are the root causes of terror? What else besides war might nations do to address these?
6. Would modern war be obsolete even without the existence of nuclear weapons? Why or why not?
7. How does the specific challenge of ending war relate to other broad planetary challenges?

NOTES

1. For representative examples, see chapter 7.
2. Thomas Jefferson, quoted in Laurence M. Vance, "Jefferson on the Evils of War," http://www.lewrockwell.com/vance/vance19.html.
3. Greg Mortenson, *Three Cups of Tea: One Man's Mission to Fight Terrorism and Build Nations—One School at a Time* (New York: Viking, 2007). See pp. 109-10 below.
4. Seth G. Jones and Martin C. Libicki, http://www.rand.org/pubs/monographs/MG741-1/.
5. http://www.mediate.com/articles/terror911.cfm. John Paul Lederach is a professor of international peacebuilding at the University of Notre Dame, South Bend, IN.
6. Robert Pape, *Dying to Win: The Strategic Logic of Suicide Terrorism* (New York: Random House, 2005).
7. In 2007, there were 658 suicide bomb attacks around the world. Of these, 542 were in Iraq and Afghanistan. See Robin Wright, "Since 2001, a Dramatic Increase in Suicide Bombings," http://www.washingtonpost.com/wp-dyn/content/article/2008/04/17/AR2008041703595.html.
8. For a conservative estimate of deaths in the Iraq war see http://www.iraqbodycount.org/database/.

9. "The World," radio program produced jointly by the BBC, Public Radio International, and WGBH Boston, April 6, 2008.

10. http://www.cbsnews.com/stories/2007/11/14/opinion/smith/main3501241.shtml?source=search_story.

11. Walter Pincus, "Waterboarding Historically Controversial," http://www.washingtonpost.com/wp-dyn/content/article/2006/10/04/AR2006100402005.html.

12. See my comments on Brzezinski, p. 70 below.

13. See Derrick Jackson, editorial, *Boston Globe*, August 1, 2007, 11.

14. Eric Lipton, "US Arms Sales Climbing Rapidly," http://www.truthout.org/article/us-arms-sales-nearly-triple-three-years.

15. Tom Regan, "Iraq is becoming 'free fraud' zone," http://www.csmonitor.com/2005/0407/dailyUpdate.html.

16. "Intelligence Work Increasingly Outsourced to Defense Firms," http://www.truthout.org/docs_2006/111007G.shtml.

17. http://www.globalsecurity.org/military/world/spending.htm.

18. Tom Englehardt, "Going on an Imperial Bender: How the US Garrisons the Planet and Doesn't Even Notice," http://www.truthout.org/article/going-imperial-bender-how-us-garrisons-planet-and-doesnt-even-notice.

19. http://www.politicsandcurrentaffairs.co.uk/Forum/u-s-forum/47734-42-2-cents-every.html.

20. Paul Stiglitz and Linda J. Bilmes, *The Three Trillion Dollar War: The True Cost of the Iraq War* (New York: W. W. Norton, 2008).

21. CBS News/*60 Minutes,* March 2, 2008.

22. John Robbins, "Terror, Love and the State of the World," in *Timeline* (publication of the Foundation for Global Community), May/June 2002, 1.

23. "Water Shortages Drive Conflicts Worldwide," http://www.truthout.org/issues_06/020808HA.shtml.

2

War Will Be Fatal Unless We Change

The unleashed power of the atom has changed everything save our modes of thinking, and we thus drift toward unparalleled catastrophe.

—Albert Einstein, 1946[1]

"THE UNLEASHED POWER OF THE ATOM"

 By far the highest of all the unacceptable costs of war is the possibility of nuclear catastrophe. While a sense of impending doom may take us only so far as a motivator of change, a dispassionate assessment of how nuclear weaponry has altered our planetary environment is essential to proving the extraordinary assertion that all war has become obsolete.

The tools of war through the ages have demonstrated a consistent increase in the efficiency of their destructive power, from the club to the spear, the cannon, the machine gun, the tank, to massive aerial bombardment.

It has been said that World War II was the last "good" war. Until 1945, war could be reluctantly rationalized as a tragic but unavoidable behavior in the difficult progress of the species toward stable international relations—though the conception of World War II as a "good" war is an American one, and not shared by most other participants. By the end of World War II, however, the invention of nuclear weapons had changed the nature of war forever.

As international power politics evolve over decades, levels of tension rise and fall. At certain moments of extremity, such as the Cuban Missile Crisis,[2] the possibility of conventional war turning nuclear became overwhelmingly real. At other times, that possibility receded so far to the back of our minds that we could hardly conceive of it happening. Our primary image of dread may have changed from mushroom clouds to planes flying into buildings. Yet all the while, the thousands of Russian and American and British and French and Chinese and Israeli and whoever else's nuclear missiles and torpedoes and artillery shells remain ready to exterminate millions.

Imagine even a limited nuclear exchange anywhere on the planet. As the rest of the world looked on, doing what little it could to alleviate the holocaust of loss, clouds of radioactive pollutants would move with the winds across borders. The entire global environment we share would be threatened. Were we still alive ourselves, we would be asking questions that examine our deepest communal values as a species. How was it that our desire for security resulted in its exact opposite, arsenals of death sprouting up everywhere that finally plunged us into unprecedented self-injury? As we drifted toward disaster, what role was played by our economic and political institutions, our definitions of self-interest, our religious convictions, our conceptions of courage, our mental stereotypes and fears?

Some might assert that concern about such a catastrophe really applies to the twentieth century's Cold War, now well behind us, and not to the twenty-first century and beyond. While history never repeats itself exactly, there is much about the instability of post–September 11, 2001, international relations that recalls the conditions leading up to the First World War. The parties who began that epic conflict almost a century ago had no idea how many millions would be killed before its four years of mindless slaughter were over. If present-day nuclear powers were to be drawn into all-out war, the same number of people could die in minutes.

It is almost impossible to get our minds around the destructive power of these arsenals. World War II took place over six years and killed more than fifty million people. The combined allied firepower of World War II, including the two atomic bombs dropped on Japan, equaled three million tons of TNT. In 1988 the firepower in the nuclear arsenals of the United States and Russia was the equivalent of *six thousand* World War IIs. Arms reduction treaties have begun to shrink this number, but not nearly enough to allow us to feel real relief.[3] At the same time, as of 2008, plans to renew the U.S. nuclear arsenal by ensuring its reliability, even with smaller numbers of warheads, have been working their way through legislative committees.[4] Many in the Congress have questioned the common sense of this project, given how hard it is to make a convincing argument that resharpening the nuclear sword would genuinely increase U.S. or global security.

Atomic weaponry now comes in many shapes and sizes, from mines and artillery shells all the way to multiple warheads, each warhead capable of a lethality that would make the destruction at Hiroshima look puny by comparison. Should such larger weapons be used on modern industrial cities, the degree of suffering simply becomes unimaginable. Systems of food and water supply, hospitals, fire stations, emergency help, all would be gone.

Scientists working with the late Carl Sagan estimated that if only 5 percent of the world's nuclear arsenals were detonated, it would cause a "nuclear winter," the effects of which could conceivably extinguish human life on the planet. Jonathan Schell cites a 2007 update of Sagan's work:

A study by Richard Turco of UCLA's Department of Atmospheric and Ocean Sciences and Owen Brien Toon, an atmospheric scientist at the University of Colorado, uses newly developed climate models to report that even a regional nuclear war in South Asia could loft enough soot into the atmosphere to severely cool the atmosphere and cripple agriculture in large parts of the globe for up to ten years.[5]

Should a nuclear war begin, it would likely grow out of just the kinds of conflicts we see in the daily headlines. While we may not like such "smaller" wars, we rationalize them as necessary, unavoidable, worth the risk. We are habituated to war as a constant backdrop to our lives, a continuous drain on our treasuries, but a necessary fallback when diplomacy fails or we don't get our way. This rationalization of war goes back through all of recorded history. War has been used to acquire, to defend, to expand, to impose, to preserve, to preempt. Each war often plants seeds for the next, in a progression that will continue until we either destroy ourselves or until we give up war.

Preventing nuclear war means preventing all war.
—Admiral Eugene Carroll, Jr., 1993[6]

Once a nuclear war did begin, it would be too late to realize that no victory was forthcoming. But, as stalemate in Korea, defeat in Vietnam, and chaos in Iraq have demonstrated, this is almost as true for modern conventional war. Because events in Iraq were set in motion irreversibly, the American and British leaders who wished to bring about a new era in the region were constrained by the unanticipated results that ensued. The preventive, nonviolent resolution of conflict is always difficult and challenging, but it is less difficult before conflict has degenerated into war than after. Prevention in today's world is worth ten-tenths, not nine-tenths, of the cure—especially in the case of potential nuclear war.

DRIFTING TOWARD THE WATERFALL

While the Cold War concepts of "balance of terror" or "mutually assured destruction" troubled our sleep for five decades, in today's multipolar world, Einstein's assertion that the unleashed power of the atom has changed everything takes on ever-more-prophetic resonance.

From the end of World War II onward, a series of historical markers has gradually confirmed that nuclear weapons are the most telling reason war is obsolete. The first marker occurred on July 16, 1945, when scientists detonated a man-made atomic explosion at Alamogordo, New Mexico. Another milestone came on August 6, 1945, when 75,000 men, women, and children died at Hiroshima, proving that humans were capable of using such awesome weapons of mass destruction against other humans. Three days later, the destruction of Nagasaki proved that Hiroshima was not an isolated anomaly. Another milestone occurred sometime in the 1950s when a second nation, the Soviet Union, gained a credible nuclear arsenal.

A further milestone was the fateful week of the Cuban Missile Crisis in October 1962, when two superpowers barely managed to avoid all-out thermonuclear war. There have been other ominous markers in recent years, such as the moment in 2001 when the United States pulled out of a foundational arms limitation agreement, the Antiballistic Missile Treaty. The bomb tests first by India, then Pakistan, then North Korea continue the drumbeat. India refuses to sign the Nuclear Non-Proliferation Treaty and seeks to enlarge its nuclear capability to maintain a balance of power against Pakistan and China. The countries of the world, absent a new agreement about our common condition, continue to be like separate individuals paddling a raft in circles as it drifts ever closer to an impending waterfall.

Far from being idealistic to say that we must end war, it is simple realism to assume that the more nations and even non-national entities that possess these weapons, the more we will be unable to escape disaster somewhere down the time stream . . . "and we thus drift toward unparalleled catastrophe."

CRACKS IN THE DAM OF DETERRENCE

The Cold War order, for all its doom-laden contradictions and icy paradoxes, now seems almost a model of clarity and

> *rationality . . . [T]he policies of the United States and the other nuclear powers have become less intelligible, less feasible, more self-contradictory, more liable to self-defeat, more drastically at odds with the basic realities of the nuclear age, and more prone to catastrophe than at any time since 1945. In consequence, the world as a whole drifts toward what some have termed "nuclear anarchy." Not since the world's second nuclear bomb was dropped on Nagasaki has history's third use of a nuclear weapon seemed more likely.*
>
> —Jonathan Schell, 2007[7]

Deterrence strategy on the part of nuclear nations has contained a paradox from the outset. In order to ensure that the weapons will never be used, they must be kept ready for instant use. We are told that the systems that keep these weapons poised on the knife-edge between readiness and safety are "fail-safe." But no such command-and-control system can possibly be entirely invulnerable to error, especially since it depends on 100 percent accuracy of interpretation of all the ambiguous signals it may receive. There is little question that the awesome power of these weapons has been a restraining force on heads of state charged with making fateful decisions. We know, however, that several U.S. presidents have considered the nuclear option, as President Nixon did, when he perceived that the United States was losing its war with Vietnam.[8] Restraint prevailed. Can we continue indefinitely counting upon the unlikely possibility that there will be no lapses of good sense, no fatal misinterpretations, among all the military forces of all the nations of the world?

The paradoxical rhetoric of deterrence quickly takes on a dangerous life of its own. The leaders of Russia or Israel or the United States, and even nuclear aspirants such as Iran, feel compelled by its logic to use the language of threat, both words and gestures, to discourage aggression in presumed adversaries. This language has the effect not only of eliciting counterthreats but also of reducing to crude, oversimplified stereotypes whole nations full of children, families, and a full human range of political and cultural opinions.

The leaders of Iran respond to superpower ultimatums by citing the double standard the major powers maintain around their own arsenals and assume that they have as much right as any other nation to possess such weapons. Nonetheless, a 2008 poll indicated that 58 percent of the Iranian people do *not* want their country to have a nuclear weapons program.[9] There is thus an opening for diplomatic initiatives based on the agreed assumption that no one could possibly "win" in a nuclear exchange between, say, Iran and Israel.

Too many people believe you have to be either for or against the Iranian people. Let's get serious. Eighty million people live there, and everyone's an individual. The idea that they're only one way or another is nonsense.

—Admiral William Fallon, former head
of the U.S. Central Command in charge
of forces in Iraq and Afghanistan[10]

It seems downright miraculous that for sixty years the world community has gotten through the inevitable close calls and misunderstandings without slipping over the edge into catastrophe. We rationalize that having the weapons is better than not having them because their strength prevents war. This assumes that deterrence will work perfectly for all countries, forever; but, given the human propensity for error, it is an empty hope.

When former Secretary of Defense Robert McNamara attended a fortieth-anniversary conference on the Cuban Missile Crisis in 1992, he was astonished to learn that the Soviets had already managed to place nuclear warheads on the Cuban mainland before the crisis began. U.S. policy makers at the time were basing their decisions upon the assumption that the warheads were still aboard blockaded Soviet vessels at sea. The United States came within a hair's breadth of launching air raids on Soviet soldiers in charge of viable nuclear missiles. An article in the *New York Times* reporting on the conference states:

> The Soviet Union had 43,000 troops in Cuba during the 1962 missile crisis, not 10,000 as reported by the Central Intelligence Agency, Robert S. McNamara said today upon returning from Havana and the final meeting of an American-Russian-Cuban series of conferences on the crisis.
>
> Mr. McNamara, who was Secretary of Defense from 1961 to 1967 under Presidents John F. Kennedy and Lyndon B. Johnson, said in an interview that Soviet officials also disclosed that they had sent Havana short-range nuclear weapons and that Soviet commanders there were authorized to use them in the event of an American invasion. The initial report appeared today in the *Washington Post*. The short-range nuclear weapons were in addition to medium-range nuclear weapons that would have required authorization from Moscow to use.
>
> The 43,000 Soviet troops were in addition to 270,000 well-trained Cuban troops, Mr. McNamara said. Expanding on views he expressed Monday, Mr. McNamara said the Soviets apparently did not expect American nuclear retaliation.
>
> "That was horrifying," he said. "It meant that had a U.S. invasion been carried out, if the missiles had not been pulled out, there was a 99 percent probability that nuclear war would have been initiated."
>
> Mr. McNamara said that the five meetings, titled "The Causes and Lessons of the Cuban Missile Crisis," which began in 1987, indicated that "The actions of all three parties were shaped by misjudgments, miscalculations and misinformation."

"In a nuclear age, such mistakes could be disastrous," Mr. McNamara said. "It is not possible to predict with confidence the consequences of military action by the great powers. Therefore, we must achieve crisis avoidance. That requires that we put ourselves in each other's shoes."[11]

The Cold War with the Soviet Union may feel like ancient history, but the United States and Russia still target each other's cities with hundreds of nuclear missiles on hair-trigger alert. Why? Because our "us-and-them" thinking remains unchanged. The mere presence of weapons on both sides creates a self-perpetuating echo chamber of mutual paranoia. Russia fears what it assumes are the nationalist/imperialist tendencies of the United States, and the United States fears similar tendencies in Russia. These fears rationalize the bureaucratic inertia that keeps our two countries from seizing the moment and going for worldwide nuclear abolition, as no less than Henry Kissinger, George Shultz, Sam Nunn, and William Perry have advocated.[12]

Meanwhile we must even live with the possibility that someone could secretly convey one of these weapons into a major city somewhere on Earth and detonate it. By comparison, such a nightmare would reduce 9/11 in all its horror to a minor incident. The thousands of warheads in the arsenals of the nuclear powers could do nothing to prevent this from happening.

As more nations want nuclear weapons in order to feel secure, those that already have them, rather than feeling more secure, feel less so—especially factoring in the possibility that any given nation might sell weapons to a rogue entity to do its bidding by proxy. The appeal of preempting adversaries becomes understandable, even overwhelming. But preemption, in its gross violation of sovereignty, only encourages the international anarchy that the community of nations devoutly wishes to avoid in the first place. Security chases its own tail.

In the larger context of moving the world beyond war, continuing to follow the precedent of preemption would be futile at best and suicidal at worst. The notion that any nation can bomb its way to a secure supply of food or water or oil, let alone security in the broadest sense, has become the ultimate in wishful thinking. Such a strategy would lead only to an endless cycle of reaction and counter-reaction, as the temporarily defeated nursed their resentments and planned ahead for opportunities to retaliate. If ever there was a moment when the family of nations had an interest in cooperating toward agreed ends, it would be the post-9/11 era. Instead, a worldwide policy of inconsistency and drift continues. In a 2007 editorial, Jonathan Schell summed up the perils associated with nuclear proliferation and the current paradigm for thinking about it:

> Previously, the United States had joined with almost the entire world to achieve nonproliferation solely by peaceful, diplomatic means. The great triumph of this effort had been the Nuclear Nonproliferation Treaty, under which 183 nations, dozens quite capable of producing nuclear weapons, eventually agreed to remain without them. In this dispensation, all nuclear weapons were considered bad, and so all proliferation was bad as well. Even existing arsenals, including those of the two superpowers of the Cold War, were supposed to be liquidated over time. Conceptually, at least, one united world had faced one common danger: nuclear arms.
>
> In the new, quickly developing, post-9/11 dispensation, however, the world was to be divided into two camps. The first, led by the United States, consisted of good, democratic countries, many possessing the bomb; the second consisted of bad, repressive countries trying to get the bomb and, of course, their terrorist allies. Nuclear peril, once understood as a problem of supreme importance in its own right, posed by those who already possessed nuclear weapons as well as by potential proliferators, was thus subordinated to

the polarizing "war on terror," of which it became a mere sub-category, albeit the most important one . . .

The good camp was assigned the job not of rolling back all nuclear weapons but simply of stopping any members of the bad camp from getting their hands on the bomb. The means would no longer be diplomacy, but "preventive war" (to be waged by the United States). The global Cold War of the late twentieth century was to be replaced by global wars against proliferation—disarmament wars—in the twenty-first. These wars, breaking out wherever in the world proliferation might threaten, would not be cold, but hot indeed, as the invasion of Iraq soon showed . . .

Vetting and sorting countries into the good and the bad, the with-us and the against-us, proved, however, a far more troublesome business than those in the Bush administration ever imagined. Iraq famously was not as "bad" as alleged, for it turned out to lack the key feature that supposedly warranted attack—weapons of mass destruction. Neither was Pakistan, muscled into the with-us camp so quickly after 9/11, as "good" as alleged. Indeed, these distinctions were entirely artificial, for by any factual and rational reckoning, Pakistan was by far the more dangerous country.

Iraq did not have nuclear weapons; Pakistan did. In 1998, it had conducted a series of five nuclear tests in response to five tests by India, with whom it had fought three conventional wars since its independence in 1947. The danger of interstate nuclear war between the two nations is perhaps higher than anywhere else in the world . . . [13]

SURVIVAL AND CHANGE

To survive, we can no longer afford to drift. We must see that our environment has changed totally and that a total change on our part is the response demanded.

Whether we find ourselves in a state of passive denial or of active concern, many assume that change on such a deep level is impossible—a nonchoice between airy utopianism and resigned acceptance of the folly of war and mass death. To overcome this pessimism, it is useful to pull back and examine our situation from the largest possible perspective.

Some four billion years ago, life emerged from the primordial mist that enveloped the Earth. Literally the descendants of stardust, primitive life forms grew in complexity and diversity. As they spread over the seas, the land, and the air, two principles remained silently at work:

- Survival and reproduction are the goal of all life. Everything that lives wants to survive—the blade of grass pushing defiantly through the pavement, the tree growing out of the granite cliff. From the single-celled amoeba to the trillion-celled human, from the sponge to the elephant, all life is driven to survive and successfully reproduce.
- The future belongs to species that adapt to a constantly changing ecological landscape, and that landscape dictates the nature of the change required. Those species that can respond to changes in the environment survive. Those that cannot adapt do not survive.

The dinosaur perfectly exemplifies these two principles. Dinosaurs ruled the Earth for millions of years as the largest, most powerful species. But when the environment changed in some fundamental way, probably as a result of the impact of a huge meteor in the Yucatan area, most dinosaur species died out. At the same time, other creatures with the ability to adapt survived. No species, however successful in the past, is guaranteed a permanent place in the interactive system of life. Survival and the ability to reproduce must be continually earned by adaptation, either genetically or behaviorally, to changes in the environment.

Eventually some mammals began to move in the direction

of less instinctual behavior, with brains evolving toward flexibility of response. About one hundred thousand years ago, *homo sapiens*—literally, "man the wise"—appeared, and these principles of survival and change moved fully into the mental dimension. We could think. We could wonder. We could ponder new possibilities. Survival no longer depended solely on genetic evolution. We humans could evolve new ideas instead. Those of us able to adapt our thinking to new environments were more fit and survived. We fashioned clothes out of animal skin that allowed us to explore new landscapes and adjust to a wider range of weather conditions. We created tools that helped us hunt more efficiently, initiating the evolution of technological prowess that led to our present tenuous dominion over all the earth.

But the two fundamental principles of survival and change still apply to the human enterprise. We are not exempt. Our changed environment dictates the change we must make to survive. We must realize that the solution lies in changing what Einstein called our "modes of thinking." We must shift from an old mode of thinking that justifies war as necessary for survival to a new mode of thinking that is based in an understanding of our interdependence with one another and our fragile life-support system.

Since the unleashing of the atom, everything to do with war—security, strength, survival, and power—has changed irrevocably. Only our thinking remains the same, rooted in millennia of waging war. Even our language is obsolete. If something can destroy millions of people in a fraction of a second, is it merely a "weapon"? If a nuclear exchange can destroy the entire life support system of the planet, is it merely a "war"? Or is this really "omnicide," the killing of everything?[14] "Friends" can no longer be clearly delineated from "foes." Urban populations worldwide are so diverse that a terrorist who detonated a weapon of mass destruction in a major city would kill thousands of his coreligionists and their children. In one of the more painful ironies of World War II, the Nagasaki bomb, having been blessed at take-off by Catholic and Lutheran chaplains, obliterated the largest Christian church in the Orient and vaporized most of its adherents.[15]

War itself has become the ultimate enemy. The only truly realistic path is to reject war—in all its forms, absolutely and forever. Because each small war contains some potential to escalate to the ultimate disaster, there are in a real sense only two possibilities behind all the complexity and nuance of international relations: continuing to wage war and moving toward our inevitable extinction, or collectively altering our course.[16]

If the word "inevitable" seems alarmist, it may help to imagine a revolver loaded with a single bullet. If the revolver has the capacity for six bullets, and we spin it, point the gun at our head, and pull the trigger, we would not have to repeat the process many times to bring about a fatal outcome. But even if the revolver with a single bullet had sixty empty chambers, or six hundred, if we keep spinning, pointing, and firing, eventually we *will* be killed. This is exactly our planetary situation when it comes to our continued reliance on weapons of mass destruction. The Cuban Missile Crisis was the equivalent of a bullet lined up in the chamber, the hammer coming down, and a near-miraculous misfire. The challenge to change comes at us much like a commandment from the Hebrew Testament: "I have set before you life and death . . . therefore choose life" (Deuteronomy 30:19). Find a way to respond creatively to new conditions—or become extinct.

When W. H. Auden was composing his great poem "September 1, 1939," in an early version he wrote the line: "We must love one another or die." Then he said to himself, "No, that's not facing the facts"; and he revised it in the finished poem to, "We must love one another *and* die." Both versions are true, but when it comes to war, Auden had it right the first time. "We must love one another or die" is a truth that has the power to compel worldwide agreement and cooperation once it is fully understood. Whether it suggests a standard that seems unreachable or the hope that is inherent in any truth, most of us do not see the issue and our own role in it that clearly and starkly. We feel paralyzed when faced with the possible destruction of our planet, either quickly by a nuclear war, or more gradually by environmental unraveling. The problem seems so big, so complex, so out of our control that our minds go numb . . . "and we thus drift . . ."

Can we stop this drift? Can we change our mode of thinking? Absolutely. We once thought human sacrifice was essential for the survival of our primitive clan. Our thinking changed and our actions followed. We eliminated the practice of human sacrifice. We once thought slavery was necessary for economic and social survival. Our thinking changed and we eliminated slavery. If there is one thing we can change, it is our minds and the way we think.

But the transition from an old to a new mode of thinking is never less than hard won. Ancient astronomers developed an Earth-centered model of the solar system that they believed to be an accurate representation of its operation. Then Copernicus broke from the mindset of his day. He saw that in reality the sun and the planets do not rotate around the Earth; the Earth and the planets rotate around the sun! Even after the astronomer Johannes Kepler made observations that proved Copernicus right, it required a long and arduous process of education to shift society's perception of the solar system from Earth centered to sun centered. Even today, we still speak casually of "sunset" and "sunrise," preserving the illusion of an obsolete reality that might more accurately, if awkwardly, be described as "turning away from the sun" and "turning toward the sun."[17]

In the same way, moving beyond war requires a demanding shift in our perception of the world—individual mind by individual mind. To ensure a future for our children and for generations to come, we must see that the world is a single, fragile life-support system where "us-and-them" thinking is obsolete. Failure to realize the implications of this interdependence will result in our going the way of the dinosaurs.

Meanwhile, it helps to remember that, in a number of significant and precious cases, precedents for the prevention of war have been established.[18] In the nuclear age, war no longer works as a way of resolving conflict primarily because, as Presidents Reagan and Gorbachev agreed in 1986, "a nuclear war can never be won and must never be fought." When people on both sides of the Iron Curtain recognized this, fifty years of Cold War ended and relations between the United States and the former Soviet Union entered a more constructive phase. The two nations shifted their thinking—from assuming that an endless arms race would enhance the security of both nations to assuming that we could work out our differences without destroying life on Earth.

Nelson Mandela's realization that only forgiveness and understanding could prevent civil war in South Africa led to the formation of Bishop Tutu's Truth and Reconciliation Commission, and to a peaceful transition out of the brutality and alienation of apartheid.[19]

In spite of such hopeful signs that humans are capable of choosing alternatives to war, building a world beyond war will be the most difficult task we have ever undertaken as a species. It is a monumental challenge. It requires changing our deepest assumptions about ourselves and what we are capable of being. Through the ages, humanity has longed for a world beyond war yet never believed it to be possible. Now it has ceased to be an impractical dream; it has become a realistic necessity.

Only after saying no to war can we discover how to say yes to re-investing ourselves and our resources in projects that address urgent security needs, such as clean water, energy, health, and adequate nourishment for all. The possession of weapons must be seen for what it is, a temporary stratagem on our path to a world beyond war, and treated accordingly. Far from viewing weapons as a temporary stratagem, our current thinking places ultimate faith in them, so we are not looking actively enough for other possibilities, even though many such possibilities are available.

The availability of these alternate stratagems, which will lead to mutually assured survival rather than mutually assured destruction, is the fourth and final reason that war is obsolete. We recall that the definition of "obsolete" implied that there was something better, and in the case of war there is. But we will not commit to a new mode of thinking and embrace such better alternatives until we become clear about the root cause of war, which is our current mode of thinking.

The conscious choice to take responsibility for the continuation of human life is further complicated by the fact that we are able to respond to it only before it happens. Since after extinction no one will be present to take responsibility, we have to take responsibility now.

—Jonathan Schell[20]

QUESTIONS FOR DIALOGUE

1. What evidence is there in history for humans having gone through fundamental changes in the past?
2. What evidence for such change can you find in your personal history?
3. Einstein asserted that everything has changed because of nuclear weapons. Do you agree or disagree? What is the "everything"? What is the change?
4. Are you convinced that if the human species continues to war, it will lead to our extinction? If not, what further information might you need to be convinced?
5. What would the international landscape look like if all countries were free to make preemptive war?
6. Will it be possible by military means to ensure that only "good guys" possess nuclear weapons and "bad guys" do not?
7. Jonathan Schell talks about "conscious choice." Whose choice?

NOTES

1. Otto Nathan and Heinz Norden, eds., *Einstein on Peace* (New York: Random House, 1981), 376.

2. See above, pp. 39-41.

3. From the Web site of the U.S. State Department: "Under the Moscow Treaty, we have agreed to reduce our operationally deployed strategic nuclear warheads to between 1,700 to 2,200, about a third of their 2002 levels, and less than a quarter of the level at the end of the Cold War. When this Treaty is fully implemented by 2012, the United States will have reduced the number of strategic nuclear warheads it had deployed in 1990 by about 80%. We also have reduced our non-strategic nuclear weapons by 90% since the end of the Cold War, dismantling over 3,000 such weapons pursuant to the Presidential Nuclear Initiatives of 1991 and 1992. Moreover, the United States introduced a new text for a Fissile Material Cut-Off Treaty on May 18, and we hope that serious negotiations can begin soon in the Conference on Disarmament. States are free, of course, to ask whether further or faster progress could or should be made, but no one can question in good faith the significant advances the United States has made to nuclear disarmament during the last two decades" (Andrew Semmel, "Is the Non-Proliferation of Nuclear Weapons Still Attainable?," http://www.state.gov/t/isn/rls/rm/67707.htm).

4. Union of Concerned Scientists, "Nuclear Weapons and Global Security," http://www.ucsusa.org/global_security/nuclear_weapons/complex-2030-does-misguided.html.

5. Jonathan Schell, *Seventh Decade: The New Face of Nuclear Danger* (New York: Holt, 2007), 15.

6. Admiral Eugene Carroll, 1923-2003, was at one point in charge of all U.S. nuclear weapons. See "Salute to an American Hero," *Timeline* (publication of the Foundation for Global Community), May/June 2003, 1.

7. Schell, *Seventh Decade*, 14.

8. Ibid., 235. "Nixon White House Considered Nuclear Options against North Vietnam, Declassified Documents Reveal: Nuclear Weapons, the Vietnam War, and the 'Nuclear Taboo,'" National Security

Archive Electronic Briefing Book, No. 195, ed. William Burr and Jeffrey Kimball.

9. http://www.worldpublicopinion.org/.

10. Quoted in Seymour Hersh, "Preparing the Battlefield," *The New Yorker,* July 7/14, 2008, 62.

11. Martin Tolchin, "U.S. Underestimated Soviet Force in Cuba during '62 Missile Crisis," http://query.nytimes.com/gst/fullpage.html?res=9E0CE7DD103DF936A25752C0A964958260&sec=&spon=&pagewanted=1.

12. Op-ed, *Wall Street Journal,* January 4, 2007 (see pp. 168-71 below for excerpts).

13. Jonathan Schell, "Are You with Us, or against Us?: The Road from Washington to Karachi to Nuclear Anarchy," http://www.truthout.org/docs_2006/111407N.shtml.

14. Adm. John M. Lee (U.S. Navy, Retired), "How a Nuclear War Might Start," Symposium on the Medical Consequences of Nuclear Weapons and Nuclear War, Lewis and Clark College, Portland, Oregon (sponsored by Portland Chapter, Physicians for Social Responsibility), April 17, 1982.

15. Dick Davis, "What If Every Church Had Been a Peace Church," http://peace.mennolink.org/articles/davis0303.html.

16. See Martin E. Hellman, "On the Inevitability of Nuclear War," Stanford University, Dept. of Electrical Engineering, preprint, 1984. See also http://nuclearrisk.org, which updates to 2008 the 1984 paper.

17. See Thomas Kuhn, *The Structure of Scientific Revolutions* (Chicago: University of Chicago Press, 1996).

18. The successful campaign in the Philippines to remove Ferdinand Marcos comes to mind, along with the Solidarity movement in Poland and the Velvet Revolution in Czechoslovakia, all three in the 1980s. The United Nations has also played a significant role in preventing war. See pp. 113-15.

19. See Njabulo Ndebele's commencement speech in appendix D, p. 172.

20. Jonathan Schell, *The Fate of the Earth* (New York: Alfred A. Knopf, 2000), 23-24.

3

The Root Cause of War

Without a global revolution in the sphere of human consciousness, nothing will change for the better in the sphere of our being as humans, and the catastrophe toward which this world is headed—be it ecological, social, demographic or a general breakdown—will be unavoidable.

—Vaclav Havel[1]

ACKNOWLEDGING OUR SHADOW

 The immediate causes of war through the ages are multiple and complex enough to fill many bookshelves with scholarly analysis. Such causes include economic, territorial, ethnic, and religious aggression—and the responses rationalized by legitimate defense—accompanied by such familiar human traits as courage, creativity, vengefulness, daring, greed, paranoia, ignorance, imperial ambition, pride, patriotic fervor, and egoism. It is easy to praise or to find fault with the protagonists and antagonists of wars through the ages. Persuasive arguments have been made to demonstrate that we would not be who we are, or would not even be here at all, were it not for the sacrifice and hard-won victory in this war or that war.

What is harder to see is the universality of the thinking that leads to war, to see it in history and to see it in ourselves. When we choose war, we think of ourselves as separate, forgetting that our fates are intertwined. We distort our adversaries into something less than human. Fear takes over. We justify and rationalize killing. The root cause of war is this old, and now obsolete, mental division of the world into "us" and "them."

The task of finding alternatives to war is made more challenging, though far from precluded, by our biological inheritance, which includes the fight-or-flight mechanisms lodged in the instinctual parts of our brains. The brains of our ancestors evolved in response to immediate threats. If they did not react quickly to an intuitive sense that a lion lay in wait a few yards away, they found themselves in grave danger of becoming lion lunch.

The threats that we face in our own time are the result of insidious changes that we cannot see right in front of us, such as gradual shifts in the global climate, or the slow but steady proliferation of nuclear weapons. To respond adequately, we need help from insights provided by the scientific study of the mind.

The illusion that we are separate, separate from one another, separate from those we think of as out-groups, and separate from the earth that sustains us, takes on more and more substance as each of us emerges from the undifferentiated condition of infancy and achieves that dynamic state of self-will we call the human ego.[2]

Our childhood sense of helplessness and unworthiness in the face of adult authority remains with all of us to some degree into our own adulthood. This half-concealed inability to fully accept ourselves causes discomfort. One way we try to relieve this discomfort is to displace our sense of unworthiness onto others. In our desire to think well of ourselves, we attempt to forge our identities in terms of what we are not. We often claim positive qualities such as kindness, honesty, and loyalty for ourselves and those like us, while we deny in ourselves and displace onto "outsiders" negative qualities such as treachery, cruelty, and dishonesty. The psychoanalyst Carl Jung called this the projection of our "shadow." In its daily manifestation, it surfaces as blame and finding fault. At its worst, projection can extend into a kind of collective mental illness, as we saw when the Nazis tried to spread their insane conception of Jews as less than human. Even today we continue to be burdened by the corrosive effects of racism, the acting out of a psychological need to define, look down upon, and fear a distinct out-group, an "other." Combine this displacement with our instinctual impulses to fight or flee, and a picture emerges of what we must acknowledge and bring to full consciousness in order to leave war behind.

When we do acknowledge our biological inheritance and our irrationalities, we can overcome our blind spots and recover our sense of the full humanity of the other—at the same time enlarging our own humanity. Jung asserted that, along with irrational blindness, there are also potentialities of great good and creativity in our unconscious, but both the exorcism of our blindness and the release of our creativity are possible only if we are willing to look closely at what we too often hide from ourselves.

In 1964, Jung defined very clearly both the universal human propensity for the alienation that results from projection, and its solution. He was speaking of the divide between the capitalist and the communist worlds, but his thoughts apply equally well in the twenty-first century to the divisiveness between the West and Islamic regions:

> We should give a great deal of consideration to what we are doing, for mankind is now threatened by self-created and deadly dangers that are growing beyond our control. Our world is, so to speak, dissociated like a neurotic, with the Iron Curtain marking the symbolic line of division. Western man, becoming aware of the aggressive will to power to the East, sees himself forced to take extraordinary measures of defense, at the same time as he prides himself on his virtue and good intentions.
>
> What he fails to see is that it is his own vices, which he has covered up by good international manners, that are thrown back in his face by the communist world, shamelessly and methodically. What the West has tolerated, but

secretly and with a slight sense of shame (the diplomatic
lie, systematic deception, veiled threats), comes back into
the open and in full measure from the East and ties us up
in neurotic knots. It is the face of his own evil shadow
that grins at Western man from the other side of the Iron
Curtain . . .

But all attempts [to resolve the problem] have proved
singularly ineffective, and will do so as long as we try to
convince ourselves and the world that it is only they (i.e.
our opponents) who are wrong. It would be much more
to the point for us to make a serious attempt to recognize
our own shadow and its nefarious doings. If we could, . . .
we should be immune to any moral and mental infection
and insinuation.[3]

To experience "our own vices thrown back in our face" in contemporary terms, we need only recall a letter that Abdul Qadeer
Khan, the nuclear engineer who later became known as the father
of the Pakistani nuclear bomb, wrote to the German magazine
Der Spiegel in 1979 in which he questioned

the bloody holier-than-thou attitudes of the Americans
and the British. These bastards are God-appointed guard-
ians of the world, to stockpile hundreds of thousands of
nuclear warheads and have the God-given authority of
carrying out explosions every month. But if we start a
modest programme, we are the Satans, the devils.[4]

In the decades subsequent to this letter, Kahn not only led a team
of scientists that allowed Pakistan to become a nuclear power, but
also apparently sold nuclear secrets and equipment to other countries. Whatever his motivation for doing this, it is tragic to think
that it was injured national pride and the feeling of being morally
patronized that led him to ignore the immorality of proliferation.
From Kahn's perspective, the West projected onto Muslim countries the colonial assumption that "we" were more responsible

stewards of weapons of mass destruction than "they," and they responded to this shadow of our unconscious condescension by producing their own bomb.

It is challenging for any country even to admit the existence of a national shadow, let alone to examine the effect it may have on others:

> Most of us don't even think about what it means to send Predators or Reapers (what a name!)—unmanned aerial vehicles—over various places to shoot off their Hellfire missiles at what's below. And even when the story comes out that it's some peasant you've hit, not the "terrorist" you theoretically aimed at, well that's "just collateral damage." And we always "regret" that. When you reverse that scenario and imagine it happening to us, Iranian pilotless drones over Southern California towns, you can see it's a nightmare and people are horrified. The US would declare war if such a thing happened to us.
>
> Unfortunately, in our world, that reversal just doesn't work most of the time. It seems too unimaginable. You can't imagine the reverse of CIA Director Michael Hayden . . . testifying before a Congressional committee and saying, "Good news! We're finally having some success infiltrating our spies into Iran." You can't imagine Ahmadinejad or the head of the Iranian secret services announcing to the Iranian press: "Good news! We've finally got our guys inside the power corridors of Washington!" Yet, when Hayden does just that in reverse, nobody blinks. Nobody thinks it's strange. And that's the degree to which our imperial view of how the world works is embedded in our national consciousness.[5]

The cultural conditioning that surrounds us like an ocean of insufficiently examined assumptions reinforces our unconscious personal conditioning.

Americans, along with people in all countries, need to ask, in the words of the Society of Friends,[6] what in our own economy, our consumption habits, our politics, and even our religious convictions might be contributing to the general condition of war. This introspective process is not easy, but it is an important retraining that will help us keep our minds clear. We can admit that our own culture's demand for illicit drugs affects conditions in Colombia or Afghanistan. We can acknowledge that both in the past and the present[7] the United States has interfered illegitimately in the internal affairs of other countries. When we do acknowledge our own misdeeds, we can take a step toward healing and understanding. Recent histories of the CIA[8] recount what many had long suspected: that agencies of the United States government did indeed try to assassinate foreign leaders and meddle in legitimate elections abroad. With such refreshing honesty, we begin to grow out of the simplistic chauvinism of "my country, right or wrong." We can go beyond schoolyard conceptions of who started it, and begin to think about the root cause of conflict and how to resolve our differences in a way that respects everyone's best interest.

After September 11, 2001, perhaps understandably given the brutality of the attack and the large number of innocent lives snuffed out on our own soil, we in the United States temporarily forgot what might have helped us keep our perspective: that terrorism is an old tactic that has been used many times by innumerable causes all over the world.[9] Yet we acted out of our shadow side in our attempts to conquer terrorism by allowing tactics such as torture and secret transport of suspects to other countries. Such actions only intensify both the ill will and the number of our adversaries and make it less likely that people who have committed crimes will be brought to justice.

We would do better to acknowledge the shadow in ourselves and our policies than to give in to the temptation to fight fire with fire. Americans and Russians, of course, find terrorism repugnant, but we conveniently forget that we each assumed we had no choice but to maintain a "balance of terror" that kept the whole planet in a state of anxiety for a half-century. The impulse to rationalize is universal: we in the United States have perfected representational government; we are a "city on a hill" with a special destiny. Other nations claim an equivalent sense of pride and uniqueness. In every case, our weapons, even though they contain the potential for mass death, are justified by the rightness of our cause. Our grandchildren will consider such methods of trying to achieve security to be as bizarre as belief in werewolves or vampires now seems to us.

We can see our instinctive fears and projections at work in the mass psychology that operates in the lead-up to war. If those in power really want a war, it is not that difficult to stir up fear and hatred, to create and demonize enemies. The techniques are well known: assert that our way of life is threatened; bring up accusations, hurts, and injustices from the past; repeat half-truths or outright lies; even fabricate events. In a prison interview, Hermann Goering, the chief of the Nazi air force, said:

> Of course the people don't want war. But after all, it's the leaders of the country who determine the policy, and it's always a simple matter to drag the people along whether it's a democracy, a fascist dictatorship, or a parliament, or a communist dictatorship. Voice or no voice, the people can always be brought to the bidding of the leaders. That is easy. All you have to do is tell them they are being attacked, and denounce the pacifists for lack of patriotism, and exposing the country to greater danger.[10]

The realities of war—death, destruction, protracted pain and suffering—are not mentioned. No solution other than war is seriously considered. The talk is only of the justifications for war and how it will be won, with massive force and brilliant strategic planning. Politicians of all parties fall into line. There is flag waving and a national rallying in support of the men and women in uniform. This is the powerful mythology of war.

The inability of each side in a conflict to acknowledge either its own negative qualities or anything positive in adversaries creates a vicious circle, as both sides descend into crude stereotyping, rationalizing ever-more-horrific cruelties. War becomes self-perpetuating as each side begins to assume that they will lose if they do not utterly annihilate the other. In the alienation that inevitably follows, language loses its clarity. The blowing up of a wedding party or the dismemberment of innocent children becomes "collateral damage." Even words that seem to have clear definitions at first, such as "terrorist" or "insurgent," become catchall terms for adversaries that supposedly "hate us for what we stand for."

Ever since the Vietnam era, television has brought war into the living rooms of the citizens in whose name the war is fought. But technology also allows a distancing and dehumanizing that makes the stark truth of war more palatable to those far from the carnage. As an editorial in the Australian newspaper *The Age* stated:

> So much talk by those pressing for an attack on Iraq is stripped bare of the bloody reality of war. It is clinical, anesthetized, and intentionally devoid of emotion . . . We are meant to ignore the fact that war is about the killing and maiming of people, about destroying their homes and communities. We are meant to ignore the fact that they are human at all, with the same hopes and fears as we have . . . We are asked to consider that they are lesser human beings who somehow deserve their fate and that their death is a reasonable price for us to ask them to pay for our objectives . . . The last Gulf War was fought without the grim, brutal reality of war ever being shown to us. It was made to look like a little boy's video game. The military control of the images, the refusal to allow the media anywhere near the action, allowed us to retain the comfortable fantasy of a war without pain . . .[11]

As we know from the plots of a thousand Hollywood movies, there is a childlike comfort in having a clear enemy that is vanquished by the end of the film. The director Clint Eastwood broke through such stereotypical "us-and-them" clichés to make two separate films about the same battle, one from the American side, *Flags of Our Fathers,* and one from the Japanese, *Letters from Iwo Jima.* These films showed the common humanity of both sides, each enmeshed in its own mythology of courage, honor, and self-defense. Eastwood did not intend a facile relativism that assumed America and Japan were equally responsible for starting the Pacific war. Instead he was encouraging the kind of understanding that might have helped the United States reflect before attacking Iraq. If the leaders of the United States had remembered that Iraqis fully share with us a sense of national pride, they might not have assumed that Iraqi citizens would welcome our soldiers after we inflicted "shock and awe" upon them.

When we refuse to oversimplify the world into black and white, the opportunity to see beyond superficial differences to the reality of human comm-*unity* presents itself. We can begin to overcome our obsolete tendency to think in terms of "you're either with us or against us" by admitting that the dualistic habit of mind is a universal human trait.

The late John Mack, a Pulitzer Prize–winning author and professor of psychiatry at the Harvard Medical School, expanded upon Carl Jung's insights in terms of more recent events:

> Listening to the pronouncements of . . . American leaders in the weeks after the events of 9/11, one could get the impression that the rage that leads to the planning and execution of terrorist acts arises from a kind of void, unconnected with history, without causation other than pure evil fueled by jealousy. Yet it is not difficult to discover that the present conflict has complex historical and economic roots. It has grown out of the affliction of countless millions of people in the Middle East and else-

where who perceive themselves to be victims of the policies of a superpower and its allies that have little concern for their lives, needs, or suffering . . .

The quest for understanding that can lead us out of our present catastrophic morass begins with the recognition that knowledge of the ways of the mind in the arenas of political conflict is relevant and useful. Political psychology is a relatively new field, but one to which not only academic psychologists and social scientists are being increasingly drawn, but also diplomats and political professionals.

The dualistic mind is not by nature self-reflective and, inasmuch as it attributes good to its own motives and actions, it will find the opposite of good in the other. Negative or aggressive ideas and feelings that are not consistent with self-regard must be pushed away, or projected outward and attributed to the enemy. A vulnerable and frightened public can all too easily be enrolled into this dangerous way of thinking. Psychologists, social scientists, spiritual leaders, and political professionals (as well as government and other institutional leaders who understand this basic truth) have a responsibility to do whatever they can in speaking and writing to change the public conversation so that the role of one's own group in the creation of political conflict can be acknowledged and examined, and new possibilities brought forth to create a genuine global community.

. . . Then we can begin to look at how the mind deals with differences, and is prone to the creation of enemies, especially when our very existence appears to be threatened. Then we can begin to look beyond mere tolerance to true knowing of the other. Only the mind that has recognized and integrated and transcended its primitive dualistic habits can begin to identify with the suffering and rage of geographically distant people. Only then can we see the aggression and ignorance that underlies our dominance and neglect, and perceive our own role in the creation of victims far from our own shores.[12]

To counter that such self-examination is "blaming America first" or defeatist beating up on ourselves is to miss the point. You and I may not be personally responsible for the crusades, or even for how the CIA meddled illegally in the Iranian elections in 1953. But by being aware of the unconscious processes that Jung and Mack invite us to examine, we can see that often it is a part of ourselves that we mistakenly hate and fear in others. We want to think of ourselves as the "white hats," the heroes who overcome evil, forgetting that, as Alexander Solzhenitsyn wrote, "The line between good and evil runs down the center of every human heart." One of the meanings of the Muslim concept of *jihad*, "self-overcoming," is based on this truth. When we move beyond "us and them," we are no longer the white hats. There is only "us," the human family, aware of our shadow, but potentially open to solutions that work for all.

COOPERATION AND WAR

By using the frontal parts of our brain, which operate out of logic and not instinctive fear-reactions, we will be freer to come up with effective answers to our many challenges. The human brain may have evolved to meet the demands of social organization. According to this theory, small groups competed with one another by developing the most efficient social integration within each group. By fostering internal cooperation, a given social unit was able to compete successfully against other social units. Thus evolved the notion of "us" and "them," with "us" being those who cooperate toward tribal survival and "them" being the enemy we seek to fend off or subdue. The society that cooperates more efficiently wins against the less-well-organized society.

Because humans have found this behavior to be an effective survival mechanism, we are habituated to this way of thinking and assume we should continue its practice into the future. "You're either with us or against us," the splitting off of the "outgroup" and thinking of them as "other," is an ancient paradigm. We assume we have to preserve war as a survival mechanism of last resort, instead of recognizing that ultimately war leads only to mutual suicide.

But humans have excelled at adapting to changing circumstances. Our nuclearized environment is telling us that our old strategy of internal cooperation must now be a universal strategy. In the past we have cooperated in limited groups to defeat our enemies and ensure our own survival. In the future we must cooperate with everyone to achieve survival for ourselves and everyone else.

We also project into our past, and onto the few remaining tribal peoples, our default assumption that our brains are fixed in the "us-and-them" mode of internal cooperation against external threats, that war has always been with us and always will be. In his book *Beyond War: The Human Potential for Peace,* the anthropologist Douglas Fry digs deeply into the archaeological past and the anthropological present and concludes as follows:

> The flexible nature of human behavior makes a transition from war to other forms of international conflict feasible. A macroscopic anthropological view reveals *Homo sapiens* to be an extremely flexible species . . .
>
> . . . Members of the same species, *Homo sapiens,* are capable of living in the dramatically different social worlds of bands, tribes, chiefdoms, and states, and within numerous cultural traditions. The transition from the millennia-old lifeways of the nomadic forager band to the conditions of the urban industrial nation is truly staggering . . .
>
> An appreciation of the immensity of social changes

that humans have undergone in recent millennia leads to the observation that there is nothing sacred about the institution of war. The worldwide archaeological record, data on simpler forager societies, and cross-cultural studies combine to suggest that warfare is a rather recent development, arising along with social complexity and greatly intensifying with the birth of states, as economic and political motives for war moved to the forefront.[13]

Fry's anthropological evidence suggests that cooperation among ever-larger groupings is as much an inbuilt potential of human nature as aggressiveness toward out-groups. In the nuclear age, all in-groups and their presumed out-group adversaries face the common threat of suicidal destruction. Our true in-group is no longer limited to a city or a nation; our in-group consists of the inhabitants of the small, fragile planet that we all share.

Humans became the dominant life form on the planet because of our ability to cooperate. For millions of years, our survival depended on cooperative hunting and the sharing of food. In an industrial economy, millions of individuals cooperate: some produce food, others mine minerals, others design machinery. Industrialized countries are massive cooperative endeavors, and we are rapidly moving from discrete national economies to one global economy.

To say that war is the dominant human behavior is like saying that the most important thing about a plane is that it can crash. The promise of a plane is in its flying, and the promise of humans, shadow and all, is in our ability to adapt to new environments and work cooperatively toward shared goals. Cooperation begins with an acknowledgment of the projection, alienation, and dualistic thinking that is the root cause of war in our own minds. It proceeds on the basis that no one and nothing is separate. The next section of the book examines this deep interdependence we share with one another and our life-support system. To understand and live the truth of this interdependence requires an open mind. Never has the adage seemed truer that our minds are like parachutes—they work best when open.

A human being is part of the whole, called by us the universe. A part limited in time and space. He experiences himself, his thoughts and feelings, as something separate from the rest, a kind of optical delusion of his consciousness. This delusion is a kind of prison for us, restricting us to our personal desires and to affection for a few persons nearest to us. Our task must be to free ourselves from this prison by widening our circle of compassion to embrace all living creatures.

—Albert Einstein

QUESTIONS FOR DIALOGUE

1. We are conditioned to believe war is caused by the evil conduct of our adversaries, as opposed to the assumption that this conditioning relies on a well-understood psychological process known as projecting our shadow side. What are the advantages of denying our shadow side?
2. What are the disadvantages?
3. How do you experience your shadow?
4. Have you experienced disliking someone and realizing that what you disliked in them was actually an aspect of yourself of which you were not fully conscious?
5. What happens when a nation projects its "shadow side" on another nation? Think of examples. What prevents this?
6. What mythological formula is common to the genesis of most wars? Are there other ingredients you would add?
7. What is your personal experience and sense of "human nature"? Do you believe people can change? If not, what do you think keeps us from changing? If so, what do you think enables change?

NOTES

1. Vaclav Havel, former president of the Czech Republic, in a 1990 address to the U.S. Congress.

2. For a comprehensive discussion of the role of ego in the present world crisis, see Eckhart Tolle, *A New Earth: Awakening to Your Life's Purpose* (New York: Penguin, 2005). Extended dialogues with Tolle on the same subject can be accessed at Oprah.com.

3. Carl Gustav Jung, *Man and His Symbols* (New York: Dell, 1985), 85, 185-86.

4. Gordon Corera, *Shopping for Bombs* (New York: Oxford University Press, 2006), 122.

5. Leslie Thatcher, "Love, Tom," http://www.truthout.org/article/leslie-thatcher-love-tom.

6. The Religious Society of Friends, also known as the Quakers, is a movement founded in the seventeenth century, many adherents of which are opposed to violence and war.

7. Seymour Hersh, "Preparing the Battlefield," *The New Yorker,* July 7/14, 2008, 60-67.

8. Tim Weiner, *Legacy of Ashes* (New York: Anchor, 2007).

9. Tony Judt, *Reappraisals: Reflections on the Forgotten Twentieth Century* (New York: Penguin, 2008).

10. Herman Goering, quoted from http://www.snopes.com/quotes/goering.asp.

11. Quoted from *Timeline* (a publication of the Foundation for Global Community), March/April 2003, 3.

12. John Mack, "Ions," *Noetic Sciences Review,* June-August 2003, 15. John Mack was a professor of psychiatry at Harvard University. He received a Pulitzer Prize for his biography of T. E. Lawrence.

13. Douglas P. Fry, *Beyond War: The Human Potential for Peace* (New York: Oxford University Press, 2007), 203-4.

PART TWO

WE ARE ONE
ON THIS PLANET

When you go around it in an hour and a half, you begin to recognize that your identity is with that whole thing. And that makes a change.

You look down there, and you can't imagine how many borders and boundaries you cross, again and again and again, and you don't even see them. There you are—hundreds of people killing each other over some imaginary line that you're not even aware of, that you can't see. From where you see it, the thing is so beautiful. You wish you could take one person in each hand and say, "Look at it from this perspective. What's important?"

You realize that on that small spot, that little blue and white thing, is everything that means anything to you. All of history and music and poetry and art and birth and love; tears, joy, games. All of it on that little spot out there that you can cover with your thumb.

—Rusty Schweickart, Apollo IX astronaut,
speech on "planetary culture" at the
Lindisfarne spiritual community

4
An Open Mind

The world is too dangerous for anything but truth and too small for anything but love.
— William Sloane Coffin, former chaplain, Yale University[1]

SEARCHING FOR TRUTH

 Each of us has a piece of the truth. Our minds filter all incoming information to conform to our internal images of our world and ourselves. While this filtering preserves the internal frame of reference to which we cling as an important component of our identity, it can hinder our quest for a more communal sense of truth. Only to the extent we test our partial picture of the truth by sharing our assumptions openly with others can we move closer (even if no final arrival is possible) to *the* truth, or closer to what is sometimes called a universal truth.

Truth is difficult for the human mind to grasp. Socrates concluded that the wisest of men are those who know how little they know. In our search for truth, we must proceed humbly, aware of the past falsehoods that we mistook for truths—the flat Earth, the geocentric universe, the malevolent influence of vampires, the economic inevitability of human slavery, the impossibility of friendship with "Red China," and now, reconciliation with those some of us may simplify into a monolithic bloc of Islamic extremists.

My separate truth in my country and *your* separate truth in your country across the water is that we are each determined to do whatever is necessary to ensure the safety of our children and grandchildren. Suddenly, in the unfolding stream of time and generations, we find ourselves each brandishing a nuclear weapon at each other to back up our desire to protect our children, and a larger truth emerges, a truth common to us both—neither of us feels secure, and only by recognizing our interdependence can we move to a place of common truth: my security depends upon yours and vice versa.

This book is built on three guiding principles: (1) war is obsolete; (2) we are one on this planet; and (3) the means are the ends in the making. This book asserts also that these principles are true—in the sense that they are not only principles, they are facts, inescapable realities of the nuclear age. As John Adams wrote, "Facts are stubborn things."

The facts are the first casualty of war, not only because the chaos of war can sweep away dispassionate journalistic assessment but also because in order to justify killing, our mental filters tempt us to let fear dominate and thus to begin to see our adversaries as less than fully human. And our adversaries do the same with us.

To survive today, we must seek truth. We must learn from our past mistakes and make new discoveries. We must come to value the differences of opinion that help us to better understand realities that are beyond the comprehension of any one mind.

As an example of truth's elusiveness in the geopolitical realm, we can reexamine what was generally perceived as a cut-and-dried act of totalitarian imperialism, the Soviet invasion of Afghanistan in 1979. Many were certain that it confirmed the evil, expansionist intentions of the Soviets. President Carter pulled the United States out of the Olympics in protest, regretting that he had been so naïve about the "Russian Bear."

Zbigniew Brzezinski, the National Security Advisor to President Carter, reminisced in a 1998 interview that the CIA began supplying the Afghans with arms six months *before* the Soviet invasion of Afghanistan, because Brzezinski hoped to draw the

Soviets into their own Vietnam-like quagmire. If this is, in fact, the correct sequence of events, Brzezinski's strategy played a part in the "blowback" that is still unfolding in headlines thirty years later.[2]

Did the invasion of Afghanistan indicate that the Soviets were bent on world domination? No. To understand why not, we must better understand how the Soviets viewed the world, whether or not we agree with their view. Over the centuries, Russia has been invaded by Mongols, Muslims, Turks, Swedes, Poles, and Austrians, leaving aside the huge invasions by the armies of Napoleon and Hitler. During World War II alone, twenty million Soviet citizens were killed. With this history, the Soviet Union had, as Russia today continues to have, an understandable, deep-seated fear concerning unrest near its borders. In the late 1970s, a militant Muslim regime had come to power in Iran, and factions in Afghanistan were, and still are, fighting to establish a similar regime there. The more recent violence in Georgia, which also borders Russia, may differ in detail but not in kind. Macho posturing on all sides, including Georgia's interest in joining NATO, led to destruction and death that did nothing to resolve the Russian perception that their "sphere of influence" had been violated, just as the United States felt in 1962 that Cuba was a threat to our strategic control of "our" hemisphere.

The Soviet invasions of Afghanistan, Chechnya, or Georgia are equivalent to U.S. reaction to unrest in Latin America. Since 1846 the United States has intervened militarily more than sixty times in South and Central America, Mexico, and the Caribbean. It assisted in the overthrow of governments in Guatemala and Chile and occupied the Dominican Republic for eight years and Nicaragua for seven. It carved out a piece of Colombia and renamed it Panama in order to create the Panama Canal. It abetted an attempted invasion of Cuba at the Bay of Pigs.[3]

The Soviet invasion of Afghanistan was not some aberration committed by a nation bent on world domination; it was the inevitable consequence of the current mode of thinking found throughout the world. This thinking justifies military intervention, however brutal and dangerous, whenever a nation believes its national security might be diminished by unrest elsewhere— or enhanced by the possession of resources elsewhere. Take the implicit assumption on the part of many American foreign policy experts that U.S. security interests would be threatened if it did not control the flow of oil from the Middle East. Then do a simple thought experiment: imagine the U.S. response if the Chinese assumed that their security interests were equally threatened if they did not control the flow of wheat from Kansas.

Commentators such as the eminent linguistics theorist Noam Chomsky have suggested that the United States has always been the archvillain of international affairs. Neither this nor the opposite view that the United States is a prince of moral virtue seems accurate. Chomsky is right that we ought to examine ourselves before we criticize the mote in another's eye. But a repeated reliance on deceit and brute force is not the practice of any one country or group; it is an old paradigm of thought common to many.

The irony of overreaching military missions that, while intended to demonstrate strength, end up revealing fundamental weaknesses is at least as ancient as the Athenian expedition to Syracuse in 415-413 BCE, when an arrogant Athenian empire undertook to occupy a distant colony and was drawn into a quagmire. All nations, like individual humans, have "shadow" areas of unconsciousness that keep them from seeing beyond obsolete definitions of their self-interest. To avoid future Syracuses, Afghanistans, Vietnams, and Iraqs we must lead the way to a new mode of thinking that recognizes that in the nuclear age these shadow areas can lead to counterproductive and potentially fatal modes of behavior.

OUR WORLDVIEW AFFECTS REALITY

Sometimes we try to apply our own certainties far outside the limited context in which they seem to us to be true, a process that the writer David Remnick has called "undergraduate universalism."[4]

One of the many tragedies of American policy in Iraq was precisely its "undergraduate universalism," defined as the assumption that our ways are the best way for everyone. In planning the invasion of Iraq, people in positions of great responsibility in the United States ignored cultural differences between Iraq and the United States, just as they also ignored desires the United States and Iraq have in common, such as not wanting to be bombed or have their sovereignty violated. U.S. leaders knew little about the infrastructure of the country they attacked and occupied, its history of tribal and religious diversity, its language and culture, its readiness for representative government imposed from without. Even in 2006, out of the thousand workers in the American embassy in Iraq, the number who were fluent in Arabic was a mere six people,[5] a measure of our indifference to the establishment of genuine cross-cultural understanding.

Tough-minded pluralism is the corrective for an "undergraduate universalism" that does not take diversity into sufficient account. Webster's defines pluralism as "A condition of society in which numerous distinct ethnic, religious, or cultural groups coexist . . ." Diane Eck of the Pluralism Project at Harvard University expands on the implications of pluralism:

- First, pluralism is not diversity alone, but *the energetic engagement with diversity.* Diversity can and has meant the creation of religious ghettoes with little traffic between or among them. Today, religious diversity is a given, but pluralism is not a given; it is an achievement. Mere diversity without real encounter and relationship will yield increasing tensions in our societies.
- Second, pluralism is not just tolerance, but *the active seeking of understanding across lines of difference.* Tolerance is a necessary public virtue, but it does not require Christians and Muslims, Hindus, Jews, and ardent

secularists to know anything about one another. Tolerance is too thin a foundation for a world of religious difference and proximity. It does nothing to remove our ignorance of one another, and leaves in place the stereotype, the half-truth, the fears that underlie old patterns of division and violence. In the world in which we live today, our ignorance of one another will be increasingly costly.

- Third, pluralism is not relativism, but *the encounter of commitments*. The new paradigm of pluralism does not require us to leave our identities and our commitments behind, for pluralism is the encounter of commitments. It means holding our deepest differences, even our religious differences, not in isolation, but in relationship to one another.

- Fourth, pluralism is *based on dialogue* [see chapter 10]. The language of pluralism is that of dialogue and encounter, give and take, criticism and self-criticism. Dialogue means both speaking and listening, and that process reveals both common understandings and real differences. Dialogue does not mean everyone at the "table" will agree with one another. Pluralism involves the commitment to being at the table—with one's commitments.[6]

Every individual on the planet brings to the table not only commitments, but also a unique frame of reference that conditions and limits his or her thinking. At the same time, not only in our hopes and dreams but even in our genes, people everywhere are almost identical.

Always remember you are absolutely unique. Just like everyone else.

—Margaret Mead

The dynamic between our precious individual uniqueness and our universal human commonality is humbling and demanding. It asks that we stay open and not be too quick to put whole categories of people into boxes. What we believe to be realistic, or even real, can be influenced for good or for ill by our unexamined assumptions.

Some cultural historians, for example, insist that our historical moment is characterized by an inevitable "clash of civilizations" between the West and Muslim regions.[7] Because "us-and-them" thinking is so pervasive and so easy to manipulate, the effect of such a conception is to make a perceived "enemy" into the mother of all stereotypes and therefore to become a self-fulfilling prophecy. We saw this at work in the West's anxiety about communism in the middle of the twentieth century, which led to ever-increasing animosity and the stockpiling of nuclear weapons. Fear-based reactions on both sides ended up creating far more danger than initially existed.

Are there people who believe that only terrorism and violence can redress perceived injustices? There are. Are some of them Islamic? Again, yes—just as some of them are Christian or Buddhist or Hindu. The survey results of Gallup pollsters John Esposito and Dalia Mogahed, assembled in their important book *Who Speaks for Islam: What a Billion Muslims Really Think*,[8] lead to some startling and counterintuitive conclusions: Muslims around the world do not see the West in stereotypic terms. They criticize or celebrate countries based on their politics, not based on their culture or religion. Muslims everywhere and non-Muslim Americans are equally likely to reject attacks on civilians as morally unjustified. Those who condone acts of terrorism are no more likely to be religious than the rest of the population. What Muslims around the world say they admire about the West is its technology and its democracy—the same top two responses given by Americans when asked the same question. And what Muslims around the world say they least admire about the West is its perceived moral decay and breakdown of traditional values—again, the same response given by Americans when posed the same question. Americans look askance at the apparent desire for the integration of religion and politics in Islamic societies, unaware that a majority of U.S. citizens also want the Bible to be a source of legislation.[9]

The future relationship between the West and the areas of the world where Muslims predominate will be conditioned by certain demographic realities. Most people in the Middle East are young: 66 percent are younger than thirty; 50 percent are younger than twenty, and 40 percent have not reached their fifteenth birthday.[10] How will these young people, vulnerable to a discontent for which their governments provide no legitimate outlet, perceive America? As a bully who makes no effort to understand their culture or speak their languages, and itself only speaks in the language of brute force? Or as a provider of medical supplies, business support, technology for clean water, and funds for universities? How can the United States refrain from behaving in ways that increase the attractiveness of extremism for the impressionable and the disenfranchised, and also increase relationship and trust? We will reap what we sow.

In the West, the blanket assumption that Islam as a whole is reflexively violent, which has gained traction since 9/11, is as illogical as stereotyping all of Christianity as inherently violent. To assume a monolithic thought pattern in hundreds of millions of people who live in countries all around the planet leads to breathtaking oversimplification. The words of a progressive Muslim scholar, Omid Safi, provide an antidote:

> Pluralism is the great challenge of the day not just for Muslims, but for all of humanity: can we find a way to celebrate our common humanity not in spite of our differences but because of them, through them, and beyond them? Can we learn to grow to the point where ultimately "we" refers not to an exclusivist grouping, but to what the

Qur'an calls the Bani Adam, the totality of humanity? Challenging, undermining, and overthrowing the pre-Islamic tribal custom of narrowly identifying oneself with those who trace themselves to the eponymous founder of a tribe, the Qur'an here describes all of humanity as members of one super-tribe, the human tribe. This is a great challenge, and yet what choice do we have but to rise up to meet it? Can we live up to the challenge issued to us by the Prophet Muhammad, and rephrased so beautifully by the Persian poet Sa'di? Can we envision each other as members of one body, to feel the pain of another as our own? . . . Muslims no less prominent than the incomparable Rumi have also echoed this emphasis on nonviolence, "Washing away blood with blood is impossible, even absurd!"[11]

Those who maintain an attitude of pluralism and goodwill stay open in their thinking about the "other" because this openness has the power to change reality for the better. In spite of genuine cultural differences, people in all parts of the world, including where Muslims make up a significant portion of the population, share much in common with those in the West. Especially they share the hope that their children can grow up to live fulfilling lives.

Because our knowledge of the world is always incomplete, true realism implies a humble reliance on discovering together what will be to the lasting benefit of all, remembering that each of us has only part of the picture. This open-minded recognition of our dual condition—uniqueness and difference nesting in a larger truth of similarity—is not weakness. It is a source of enormous strength. The possibility of open minds sharing their commitments with one another in the context of a common destiny can change reality because it initiates a positive dynamic built on mutual self-interest—the recognition that we are one on this planet.

You can't assert yourself in the world as if nobody was there. Because this is not a clash of ideas. There are people attached to those ideas. If you want to live without violence, you have to realize that other people are as real as you are.

—Clifford Geertz[12]

QUESTIONS FOR DIALOGUE

1. Is truth absolute or relative? Can we come closer to truth? How?
2. What happens when we approach life with an open mind? Does it mean we have to give up our convictions?
3. Is there a difference between tolerance and active engagement with diversity? What is the difference?
4. Do you believe that our worldview changes or can change reality? Why or why not?

NOTES

1. See http://brainy quote.com/quotes/quotes/w.williamsl0111419.html.

2. http://www.proxsa.org/resources/9-11/Brzezinski-980115-interview.htm.

3. See Stephen Kinzer, *Overthrow: America's Century of Regime Change from Hawaii to Iraq* (New York: Times Books, 2007).

4. David Remnick, "The Apostate," *The New Yorker,* July 30, 2007, 34.

5. James A. Baker III and Lee H. Hamilton et al., *The Iraq Study Group Report* (New York: Filiquarian, 2006), 92.

6. Diana Eck, The Pluralism Project, http://www.pluralism.org/pluralism/what_is_pluralism.php.

7. Samuel P. Huntington, "The Clash of Civilizations?," http://

www.foreignaffairs.org/19930601faessay5188/samuel-p-huntington/the-clash-of-civilizations.html.

8. John Esposito and Dalia Mogahed, *Who Speaks for Islam: What a Billion Muslims Really Think* (New York: Gallup, 2008).

9. Ibid., 49.

10. Alan Richards, political economist and professor of environmental studies, University of California, Santa Cruz, quoted in *Timeline* (publication of the Foundation for Global Community), September/October 2002, 6. Six years later the exact figures are obviously becoming dated, but the general point remains valid.

11. Omid Safi, *Progressive Muslims: On Justice, Gender, and Pluralism*, ed. Omid Safi (Oxford: Oneworld Publications, 2003), 140. Cited with permission.

12. Clifford Geertz, anthropologist and professor emeritus at the Institute for Advanced Study, Princeton, NJ.

5

Interdependence

Once a photograph of the whole earth from space becomes available . . . a new idea as powerful as any in history will be let loose.

—Fred Hoyle, astronomer[1]

YOUR FATE IS MY FATE

 Einstein voiced his prophetic insight about the grave danger of nuclear proliferation ("The unleashed power of the atom has changed everything . . .") in 1946. Only a few years later, Fred Hoyle thought ahead to the possibility that photographs taken by astronauts would help us experience on the gut level the scientific truth that the whole Earth is a single system—and that this understanding could fundamentally expand and change our thinking. As a Peace Corps volunteer once said, "The Earth is a sphere, and a sphere has only one side. We are all on the same side." From this enlarged perspective, it is possible to see that what we humans have in common can outweigh the differences that often have led us to war.

In a nuclear world, the question of whether we hate our enemies more than we love our children has become more than a clever bumper sticker. Our fates are enmeshed with one another and with the dynamic interaction of air and water and soil without which we cannot live. Whatever enhances or diminishes your security and well-being does the same for me. Such thinking has just as much potential appeal to anyone we might consider an adversary as it does to us. This ethic of interdependence is confirmed in the variations of the Golden Rule that are found in all the world's religious traditions:

> Buddhism: Hurt not others in ways that you yourself would find hurtful.
>
> Hinduism: Do naught unto others what would cause you pain if done unto you.
>
> Judaism: What is hateful to you, do not to your fellow man.
>
> Christianity: Do unto others as you would have them do unto you.
>
> Islam: No one of you is a believer until he desires for his brother that which he desires for himself.
>
> Sikhism: I am a stranger to no one; and no one is a stranger to me. Indeed, I am a friend to all.
>
> Taoism: Regard your neighbor's gain as your own gain and your neighbor's loss as your own loss.

In these different ways of stating the principle of interdependency, we find one of the most profound points of agreement among the various wisdom traditions that have come down to us from the ancient world.

UNITY AND INTERDEPENDENCE

The deepest context for moving beyond the "us-and-them" thinking is found in the unity principle that pervades all scientific disciplines and much religious thought. The ancient peoples of the Middle East had an intuition of this unity when they gradually gave up their polytheism in favor of a belief in one God. And a cornerstone of Buddhist doctrine since ancient times has been the interdependency of all things and beings. Nothing, including ourselves, exists or has functional significance apart from everything else.

Scientists and theologians may disagree on the ultimate meaning of this unity principle, but they can agree on some basic premises. The universe preceded our religious texts and beliefs. It elicits awe and wonder, confounding inquiry by posing new questions for every one that we answer. It is dynamic, in process, always changing. We emerged from it, and we are subject to its laws: we are one with it. Nothing is isolated.

In current theories of physics, matter is not seen as autonomous particles acting and reacting against one another. Rather, matter exists as a network of relationships, more like a wave. All matter in the universe is connected like a circle of fine thread. Every single atom is in communion with every other atom in the entire cosmos. If any part moves, it sends a wave around the circle, back even to the part that started the movement. The actor is also acted upon. Everything is so interconnected that even observation affects the nature of what is being observed.

Lift your little finger and the stars move—ever so slightly, but they move. When the stars move, you are affected—ever so slightly, but you are affected. The same law of gravity that governs planetary motions and the formation of galaxies is present down to the subatomic level. The unity principle is present in its very name, the law of *universal* gravitation. The basic forces of the universe link everything to everything else.

Similarly, no one person and no nation can exist in isolation. The concept of an individual or nation acting separately is an illusion. As in physics, the actor is always acted upon: we are part of one unified whole. This principle of unity becomes more evident with each new realization that all our significant ecological challenges are transnational and transreligious. There is only one atmosphere, only one vast ocean circling the globe. Life on Earth is like one gigantic organism, with the various species constituting its organs and cells.

If we disrupt this single system in one place, it can create unpredictable and sometimes undesirable effects in another. On the island of North Borneo, prior to 1955, malaria affected 90 percent of the people. A pesticide similar to DDT was sprayed to kill the malaria-carrying mosquitoes. It eliminated the mosquitoes, and, in an unforeseen side effect, also killed the flies that infested the houses. At first this was welcomed as an extra benefit. But then lizards began to die from eating pesticide-laden flies. Next, cats died from eating the lizards. With the cats gone, a large rat population emerged from the jungle, teeming with typhus-ridden fleas, and overran the village. Fortunately this situation was resolved without an epidemic of typhus, but the lesson of interconnection is universal.[2]

What strengthens the health of the Earth strengthens our own health. What weakens whole ecosystems weakens us. No sentient human can avoid the overwhelming evidence of the cause-and-effect interaction between ourselves and the total planetary system of life. The size of our personal carbon footprint may be causing typhoons or increases in sea level that could be fatal to our fellow humans on the other side of the Earth. Hormone-affecting chemicals from the manufactured materials that furnish our homes have been found in human breast-milk. In the most remote reaches of the world's oceans, scientists find birds, turtles, and fish that have died from having eaten or become entangled with the waste of our consumer culture. Manufactured chemicals have worked their way down temperate rivers into ocean currents and spread to arctic regions where they infuse the blood of polar bears.

Ecology and biology also teach us less cautionary and more optimistic lessons about the unity principle. The ecosystem derives strength from its diversity, both the many different species and the differing genetic makeup of individual organisms within a species. When a diverse system is faced with environmental stress, it has more ways to respond and adapt.

The same principle applies to the social dimension as well. Diversity of culture is often viewed as threatening and divisive when in fact it is an essential source of strength and adaptability. By combining our diverse viewpoints we can obtain a more accurate picture of the challenges we face. Only then will we find creative solutions to our problems, especially the overarching problem of planetary sustainability.

Biology has also shown that, in an interrelated system, survival of the fittest does not necessarily mean survival of the strongest. No longer is the evolution of life seen only as a bloody battle between competing species where the fit are the biggest, strongest, and most aggressive. Participants in an ecological system are fit if they make a contribution to the whole system and at the same time allow future generations of their species to survive and reproduce.

As evidence, the most diverse, abundant, and oldest form of life is one we cannot see with the naked eye, the single-celled organism. Without single-celled organisms, the diversity of life would not be possible. Between 70 percent and 80 percent of the oxygen in the Earth's atmosphere is produced by single-celled marine algae. Single-celled organisms are the Earth's most important contributor to decomposition, renewing the old to make material available to the new. Unless single-celled bacteria inhabited the stomachs of cows and other livestock, these animals could not digest the cellulose in grass and create protein critical to the survival of societies where plant-based protein is less available.

Diversity is fueled by symbiotic relationships between organisms. Many species cannot survive without each other. Consider zooxanthellae, microscopic algae that can live only within the animals that form coral. In equatorial waters otherwise devoid of life, zooxanthellae produce sugar through photosynthesis, feeding their coral hosts. In exchange, the zooxanthellae are provided with a place to live.

We are all connected by the constant passage of energy from organism to organism. Virtually every species of life on Earth derives energy from the sun. Photosynthesis begins the process of transforming this solar energy into the myriad of forms that fuel the living system. All of us, from the smallest cells to the largest living mammals, exist only by means of the heat we receive from our nearby star.

Our biological interconnectedness is also manifested through the passage of time. We are made from matter that flared forth at the creation of the universe. Any species at any given moment is temporarily borrowing material that has evolved through an unfathomable number of living and nonliving manifestations over billions of years. And in order for us to be here today, every one of our ancestors all the way forward from the first living organisms had to successfully reproduce before they died. We ourselves, even as we threaten one another with our stockpiles of omnicidal weapons, contain the still unfolding potential of this success story of survival and change.

In the unity principle, we see our situation in space and time as it really is: we are part of one shining, fragile, and beautiful planet, with one life-support system. Our future depends on our acting from a new mode of thinking based in this reality—a reality that contains the seeds of a new hope for our species. As Barbara Ward and Rene Dubos remarked,

> It is even possible that recognition of our environmental interdependence can do more than save us, negatively, from the final folly of war.
>
> It could, positively, give us that sense of community, of belonging and living together, without which no human society can be built up, survive, and prosper.
>
> Our links of blood and history, our sense of shared culture and achievement, our traditions, our faiths, are all precious and enrich the world with the variety of scale and function required for every vital ecosystem. But we have lacked a wider rationale of unity. Our prophets have sought it. Our poets have dreamed of it.
>
> But it is only in our own day that astronomers, physicists, geologists, chemists, biologists, anthropologists, eth-

nologists, and archeologists have all combined in a single witness of advanced science to tell us that, in every alphabet of our being, we do indeed belong to a single system, powered by a single energy, manifesting a fundamental unity under all its variations, depending for its survival on the balance and health of the total system.

If this vision of unity—which is not a vision only but a hard and inescapable scientific fact—can become part of the common insight of all the inhabitants of planet Earth, then we may find that, beyond all our inevitable pluralisms, we can achieve just enough unity of purpose to build a human world.[3]

EXPANDING OUR IDENTIFICATION

The image of the whole Earth from space with no visible borders has expanded our minds and spirits in a way that cannot be reversed. It may not make the particulars of our local and national decisions easier, but it reorients our collective reality within an all-encompassing perspective.

When we shift from the illusion that war, however distasteful, will lead to our survival, to the reality that war will lead to our extinction, the notion of "we" expands. This more inclusive "we" means everyone on Earth, not just the national "we." Until recently, for all of the human species, the meaning of "we" was far narrower, more exclusive. We had limited experience of other peoples and other cultures. Therefore, our primary loyalty was limited to our family, tribe, race, religion, ideology, or nation. That loyalty is an important part of our identity. It shapes our values, our attitudes, our motivations, and our actions. But because our identification has been restricted, separating cooperating in-groups from unfamiliar out-groups, we, in justifying war, have often seen those beyond that identification as our enemies.

The process of expanding our identification happens natu-

Figure 1. Expanding Our Identification

rally in the course of our lives. When we are infants, the mental circumference of our world is restricted, encompassing only our basic needs for our next meal or a dry diaper. As we grow, this limited world expands. We realize we are part of a particular family, living in a particular town, attending a particular school, for whose side we root in competitive sports. On the collective level, we discover our loyalty to our country or our identification with a particular ethnic background. In terms of ideas, we begin to identify on a collective level with a specific ideology, philosophy, or religion. We can easily feel angry or hurt if these identifications are criticized, threatened, or attacked.

While we will always see ourselves as part of a particular family, race or nation, now our broader identification must be with all humanity, all life, the whole Earth. We must no longer be preoccupied with enemies, dividing the world into "us" and "others." We can no longer see ourselves as separate. In an age of weapons of mass destruction and global ecological stress, this limited identification threatens all of humanity.

We will never eliminate disagreements between individuals or nations. But different perspectives, different ideas, and different approaches to problems can become a source of creative solutions. An overriding identification with the whole Earth will enable us to resolve conflicts without violence. This does not mean we need to give up the identifications that formed us, but it does mean we must understand them within their larger context.

Our global ecological challenges only accelerate the expansion of our identities demanded by the world-destroying weapons we have invented. We must now see that we share a common destiny.

The only viable context for future survival seems to be . . . the planet Earth and its integral functioning as a controlling referent. Only such a referent to the Earth itself, beyond all the various nations of the planet, can evoke a sense of common future. There needs to be a realization that no nation has a future if the planet does not have a future.

—Thomas Berry[4]

Our individual well-being depends on the well-being of the whole system. This need for empathy with one another and all the living forms of Spaceship Earth suggests a third basic principle necessary to living beyond war that derives from the first two, war is obsolete and we are one. No longer can illusory notions of separate self-interest justify violent means. Instead, the means are the ends in the making.

QUESTIONS FOR DIALOGUE

1. Humans traditionally view ourselves as living in an "us-and-them" world, as opposed to seeing that this view is an illusion—that there is only "us" and that if we fail to realize that we are one we will destroy ourselves. In what ways do you see we are one?
2. In what ways do you disagree that we are one?
3. What evidence supports the conclusion that we are one?
4. What evidence supports a contrary view?
5. How does the "globalization" of our challenges change the meaning and implications of the Golden Rule?
6. What does the unity principle mean to you? What was your earliest experience of it? How have you experienced it since?
7. How is the unity principle connected to the assertion that war is obsolete?
8. What happens to your limited identification when you expand your identification to include all people and the whole Earth? Can you still be an American, Iranian, or Australian? A Buddhist, Jew, Muslim?
9. How can a more inclusive identification change what is real, realistic, or possible?

NOTES

1. Sir Fred Hoyle, *The Nature of the Universe* (London: Blackwell, 1950), 9-10.
2. G. Tyler Miller, Jr., *Living in the Environment*, 2nd ed. (Belmont, CA: Brooks Cole, 1979), 92.
3. Barbara Ward and Rene Dubos, *Only One Earth: The Care and Maintenance of a Small Planet* (New York: W. W. Norton, 1972), 77.
4. Thomas Berry, *Evening Thoughts*, ed. Mary Evelyn Tucker (San Francisco: HarperCollins, 2006), 84.

PART THREE

THE MEANS ARE THE ENDS IN THE MAKING

We must be the change we want to see in the world.
—Mahatma Gandhi

6

Living Beyond War

One day we must come to see that peace is not merely a distant goal we seek, but that it is a means by which we arrive at that goal. We must pursue peaceful ends by peaceful means.
—Martin Luther King, Jr.[1]

 If war is obsolete and we are one on the planet, a third guiding principle logically follows: the means are the ends in the making. We can no longer allow the ends to justify the means. This has implications on every level from the personal to the international. The present chapter explores the personal implications of the congruency of means and ends, while chapter 7 considers some possible international implications of that congruency.

We cannot advocate for peace between countries yet to be at war with our families, our neighbors, our colleagues, or our own government. What are the behavioral implications of expanding our identification to encompass all humanity and the whole Earth? What means can we choose that are aligned with our ultimate goals? Three core practices will allow us to live our individual lives consistently with the overarching principles necessary to build a world beyond war: (1) resolving conflict; (2) maintaining goodwill; and (3) working together.

I WILL RESOLVE CONFLICT.
I WILL NOT USE VIOLENCE.

The first core practice is a commitment to resolve conflict without physical or psychological violence. "Resolve" comes from the Latin *solvere*, "to untie," "to release," and is related to words such as "dissolve" and "solution."

Most conflicts are not truly resolved. Despite the growing influence of effective school conflict resolution programs, the vast majority of us have not been trained to resolve conflict.[2] Instead we try one of several unsatisfactory approaches.

The usual response is a nonresponse: we ignore conflict, hoping it will go away. But it only simmers, waiting to boil up again later. Once in the midst of conflict, we often debate or fight, each party trying to impose its will on the other psychologically or physically. The conflict appears to be resolved when one party prevails. But the defeated, whether in war or domestic argument, often nurse their smoldering bitterness, hoping to take revenge or prevail at another time. If neither party is strong enough to impose its will, the conflict may be temporarily suppressed, only to emerge with renewed force sometime in the future.

The techniques of conflict resolution are well understood. Attack the problem, not the person. Listen actively. Cooperate together to solve the problem fairly. Look for options where both sides can win. Concentrate less on the outcome we want, and more upon why we want it, which often opens up solutions.

The classic story to illustrate this describes two sisters fighting over the only orange in the family larder. Each sister must have the entire orange for herself, any less is impossible. A wise parent asks each of the girls why she wants the orange. One explains she wants to drink the juice; the other wants to use the rind to cook a pudding. What each sister wants is her position, why she wants it is her interest. In this case, the simple solution is to give the cook the rind after the juice has been squeezed for the thirsty sister—thus meeting the interests of both.[3]

If only the resolution of all conflict could be so elegant! But a solution presented itself, as it often does, on the level of *interests:* interests revealed by asking *why* the opposing parties each want what they want.

No matter how many conflict-resolution techniques we acquire, the primary issue is our motivation, our attitude. We must be courageous enough to face conflict, dedicated enough to stay with it until it is resolved, and open-minded enough to allow that to happen.

Violence can never resolve the underlying source of conflict; therefore, we cannot use violence of any kind. Our means must be consistent with the peaceful result we want. Until we decide to reject violence as a means of "resolution," we will not discover and practice the alternatives to violence that are available.

Because conflict is challenging and uncomfortable, it is almost always perceived negatively. But if we see conflict as an opportunity to walk in another's shoes, its meaning changes. True resolution of conflict results in understanding on a new level, a deeper connection between spouses, colleagues, or nations. With practice, we can choose to see conflict as an opportunity for mutual caring, sharing, and learning. Martin Hellman writes:

> I will never forget the day my wife, Dorothie, told me that I had to love her even when she was angry. Going further she informed me that at such times I had to love her, not in spite of, but because she was angry. After my initial shock and resistance, I realized that, while it was extremely uncomfortable for me when she was angry, I would not eliminate her angry times even if I could— which of course I could not. Many things that she needed to say, and I needed to hear, only came out when she was angry. I later came to see another benefit of Dorothie's

demand: I could ask her for the same consideration, and was thus able to be heard in a way that before had seemed impossible.

As we learned to hear each other better, we came to see that our anger was usually a result of not having been able to say things that needed to be said, or not having been adequately heard. Once we could express ourselves and be heard, the anger had less chance to build.[4]

The most difficult challenge in building a world beyond war is the obvious one: what can I do when *I* am ready to resolve a conflict nonviolently, when *I* feel willing to work out a solution that benefits all parties, but my adversary does not appear to be similarly motivated? This situation is not an excuse to abandon the decision to seek nonviolent resolution. It is the very occasion where this decision is most needed. If I remain 100 percent committed to a nonviolent resolution, we could be at least 50 percent of the way there.

My adversary may be aggressive because of his fear that I may destroy him unless he destroys me first. If I am free to choose a creative response and he seems too frightened or angry to be able to consider alternatives with me, then I bear even more responsibility to offer solutions that deescalate the crisis. This is how police are trained to respond—unlike armies.

We must develop and maintain the capacity to forgive. He who is devoid of the power to forgive is devoid of the power to love. There is some good in the worst of us and some evil in the best of us. When we discover this, we are less prone to hate our enemies. Forgiveness is not an occasional act; it is a permanent attitude.

—Martin Luther King, Jr. [5]

This does not imply a purely pacifist response, only an intelligent and creative one. We can remain prepared to defend ourselves against violence while we explore less force-oriented and more confidence-building solutions. If an insane person is rampaging through a school, we are grateful to have well-trained police who may have to subdue the perpetrator before others are harmed. Even if we fail to prevent the worst, we can respond to it with compassion for human fragility rather than vengefulness. When the Amish in Nickel Mines, Pennsylvania, took food to the family of the mentally ill man who had murdered five young women at their local school, it was reported as admirable but eccentric; rather, it was a profoundly mature response to tragedy.

I WILL MAINTAIN AN ATTITUDE OF GOODWILL. I WILL NOT PREOCCUPY MYSELF WITH AN ENEMY.

The second core practice is to commit to maintain an attitude of goodwill. It is important to define goodwill clearly, because, like the commitment to resolve conflict without violence, it does not imply a set of techniques but a shift in attitude. The shift is away from an egocentric view of the world and toward a view that encompasses whole situations and all parties' interests. This willingness to set aside our ego is the polar opposite of passivity. It means freeing ourselves from the wasted energy of righteous indignation and blaming in order to be able to act as creatively as possible.[6]

Maintaining an attitude of goodwill requires setting aside blame. Blame muddies the already-swirling waters of conflict and reduces our ability to see our situation clearly at a challenging moment. When we assume that the other party is entirely responsible for the conflict, we give away not only our own responsibility but also our own receptivity to solutions and freedom to initiate.

Therefore, we should not preoccupy with those we think of

as enemies—not the Iranians, nor the president, nor candidates from the party we oppose in an election, nor anyone we think is making our lives difficult. Instead, we should focus on what we can do to help bring about solutions. Len Traubman[7] compares the ever-demanding task of keeping our own attitude inclusive and positive to keeping a beach ball underwater—without constant effort to keep it down, it pops back up. Without constant effort, we pop backward from responsibility to blame.

Responsibility goes way beyond "being nice." It means having the authenticity to bring up a perceived conflict when politeness, fear, or wanting our own way suggests that we ignore it. At the same time it means being inclusive, in the sense of being open and present to the "other" who is opposed to us. Far from allowing ourselves either to bulldoze or be bulldozed, the exercise of maintaining goodwill calms our instinctive temptation to fight or to flee. We may be flooded with negative feelings at a moment of acute conflict with a boss, colleague, spouse, or child, yet remain willing to listen to the other. The ability to listen is an acquired skill, one that gets better with practice, but it begins with an attitude shift.

Maintaining an attitude of goodwill toward someone means having a deep and active caring for that person's well-being. It requires a conscious choice to identify with the larger whole, even in a conflict—especially in a conflict! What is best for spouses as a couple? For children as part of a family? For the country as part of the family of nations?

It can be hard to recognize when we bear ill will toward others. Whenever someone else is disturbed—especially if they disagree with us—and we have little sympathy for their predicament, we need to recognize that we bear ill will. We then have the opportunity to move from acting from the fear-based part of our brains to acting from our conscious and rational forebrains, from ill will to goodwill, from blame to responsibility, from problem to solution.

Established brain research has shown that goodwill and ill will are two mutually exclusive modes of being.[7] The brain cannot feel both at the same time. If we have an attitude of ill will, we add to the hostility and alienation already present on the planet; we are part of the problem. If we maintain an attitude of goodwill, we become catalysts for positive change.

I WILL WORK TOGETHER WITH OTHERS TO BUILD A WORLD BEYOND WAR.

A third core practice is to learn to work together on a whole new level, with an attitude of open consultation. Together we can accomplish far more than we ever could working alone. The task is educational, both to model a new way of thinking and to build agreement about it in the world. A change this extensive requires the direction, organization, and cooperation of many people working effectively together, challenging and supporting one another.

This level of collaboration requires not just tolerance but the celebration of difference. Successful conflict resolution in its very essence depends on a shift in attitude from opposing difference to embracing it. While Americans, for example, have enjoyed the benefits of an ongoing influx of diverse cultural frames of reference through our immigration policies, we have also historically held the melting pot as our image of how difference should be incorporated. We have viewed foreigners as outsiders until they are properly melded into our own homogenous totality both in language and social custom.

But embracing difference does not mean throwing it into the melting pot to be realigned to fit the general view. It means genuinely and actively valuing difference. A view different from one's own is not necessarily wrong or threatening. It is instead a blessing, because it presents us with an opportunity to learn. What assumptions have led the other person to his view, and what assumptions have we embraced in coming to our view? What interests do we have that our view serves and what interests does the other person have that are served by that view? Am I in illusion, or are we both in illusion, and a third view makes more sense? How can we explore these differences together to understand what is true? How can we honor one another's views until all is fully understood?

Yes, you say, but I'm certain I'm right and he's wrong. History is full of examples where those who knew they were right were wrong, and the person everyone knew was wrong was actually right. Galileo comes to mind. Even though we believe deeply that something is true, we may be in error. In addition, someone who holds an incomplete and incorrect truth in his heart usually can discover something new only if others are willing to explore that truth with him, rather than trying to force him to accept another view.

We are all imperfect processors of information. Our minds can explore the mass of data confronting us only by creating assumptions and then organizing the data based on those assumptions. That is what the ancient Greeks did with splendid accuracy when they hypothesized the Ptolemaic universe with the Earth at its center. Having assumed that the Earth was the center of the universe, they made the data they possessed about the solar system fit that assumption. We ourselves often proceed under false assumptions, and we, too, are often tempted to manipulate data to support them, as the United States did in the misinterpretation of intelligence data that rationalized the Iraq war. We must be alert to the possibility that our assumptions are wrong and be willing to modify the assumptions rather than rework the data. Therefore difference, far from being something we should fear, is of supreme value. Together we can uncover misconceptions and reach results that serve our mutual interests.

The meaning of working together has an even-deeper dimension. Not only should we not impose solutions on others, but also we need to see the dynamic opening toward growth that is inherent in all relationships, an opening that is the ultimate active extension of the Golden Rule.

Working together with people in a spirit of goodwill and no blame can bring out the best in ourselves and others, in a way that strengthens all of us. We are familiar with how this works in parenthood, where the needs of a child bring forth new strengths and skills from parents that they can use to help the child grow. We see this same relationship in good teaching, where the eager curiosity of the student brings out the best that a teacher has to give. In each case, the actor is acted upon.

These core practices of living beyond war represent an unprecedented shift in human behavior, matched only by the unprecedented threat to our survival that war poses today. Only a few rare individuals in human history have been able to hold faithfully and consistently to such practices. The three guiding principles and three core practices redefine what peace really is: not merely the absence of war and terror, but an active, never-ending effort. If we really want peace, we must acknowledge that peace, on every level, takes just as much preparation, training, cooperation, and vigilance as war.

The future of the world depends on millions of people understanding and acting on the belief that alternatives to violence and war will lead to the kind of world we all want for ourselves and all our children. The next chapter lays out some of the ways these alternatives are as useful and practical for resolving international conflicts as they are for personal ones.

Look, peace is not just sitting there peacefully, right? Peace is active. Peace means you have to care about people and do things actively to promote that care. It's not just saying I won't go to war. It's saying I'm going to do something to prevent it, you know? And here's what I'm going to do. Peace is not a state. It's the result of an activity, and many activities ...

—George Lakoff[8]

QUESTIONS FOR DIALOGUE

1. Can all conflict be resolved without violence?
2. Think of examples of situations where conflict is increasing in our world. Are there creative ways to resolve these situations without violence?
3. Think of a conflict in your life that was not resolved. Could it have been resolved? How?
4. Think of a conflict in your life that was resolved. What did "resolution" mean? Was it complete?
5. Can you blame and be in a state of goodwill at the same time?
6. What has happened in your own life when you have not maintained goodwill? When you have preoccupied yourself with an enemy? When you have casually expressed your dislike of a given candidate running for office?
7. How are working together effectively and appreciation of difference connected?

NOTES

1. Martin Luther King, Jr., "A Christmas Sermon," December 24, 1967, in *Where Do We Go from Here: Chaos or Community?* (Boston: Beacon, 1968), 45.

2. http://education.ufl.edu/web/?pid=305; www.pbis.org; and www.cfchildren.com are Web sites for programs and curricula for helping children learn conflict resolution skills.

3. www.negotiationskills.com/articleB1.php. Steven P. Cohen, president of the Negotiation Skills Company in Pride's Crossing, MA.

4. Martin Hellman, "Resist Not Evil," http://ee.stanford.edu/~hellman/opinion/Resist_Not.html.

5. *The Words of Martin Luther King, Jr.,* ed. Coretta Scott King (New York: Newmarket, 2001), 13.

6. For a profound discussion of moving beyond egocentricity, see

Eckhart Tolle, *A New Earth: Awakening to Your Life's Purpose* (New York: Penguin, 2005).

7. http://www.blogtalkradio.com/DemocracyForAmerica/2008/07/17/DFA-Night-School-Framing-the-2008-Election. During this lecture, George Lakoff discusses the binary nature of neuronal transmission.

8. Ibid.

7

Far Better Than War

In an era of nuclear missiles and other weapons of mass destruction, trying to achieve security through the threat or use of military force is like trying to perform heart surgery with a chain saw.

—Douglas Fry, anthropologist[1]

 If war is obsolete and we are one on the planet, we cannot get to a world beyond war by using war. Instead, our nation's policies and actions should reflect the principles and compassion of our citizens. But citizens need more information about alternatives to war that people and nations can turn to with confidence. Because our media rarely talks about them, most of us find it hard to see that there are plenty of effective models for resolving conflict that work better than war. Many options are available that allow us to increase our own security by inviting adversaries to work with us toward common security goals—without unilaterally abandoning our own military strength. Four basic, interrelated strategies that will help prevent and end war are:

- the practice of diplomacy and nonviolent conflict-resolution processes
- the contribution of appropriate humanitarian foreign aid to developing countries
- respect for and adherence to international law
- cooperation and collaboration with other nations.

DIPLOMACY AND NONVIOLENT
CONFLICT-RESOLUTION PROCESSES

Many examples already exist of effective international diplomacy, dialogue, negotiation, and other nonviolent conflict-resolution processes. When apartheid ended in South Africa, the international community expected a bloodbath. It didn't happen. The Truth and Reconciliation Commission, led by Nelson Mandela and Bishop Desmond Tutu, brought perpetrators and victims together in a way that allowed forgiveness, justice, and healing.[2]

Bishop Tutu writes:

It was the Commission's goal to reach out to as many South Africans as possible, offering amnesty to all, both to those who had been victims and those who had been perpetrators during apartheid's long reign. Our slogan was: The truth hurts, but silence kills . . .

At first we feared that few would come forward, but we need not have worried. We ended up obtaining more than twenty thousand statements. People had been bottled up for so long that when the chance came for them to tell their stories, the floodgates opened . . . And then you heard their stories and wondered how they had survived for so long carrying such a heavy burden of grief and anguish so quietly, so unobtrusively, with dignity and simplicity. How much we owe them can never be computed.

What a spectacular vindication it has been, in the struggle against apartheid, to live to see freedom come, to have been involved in finding the truth and reconciling the differences of those who are the future of our nation.[3]

More than thirty truth commissions, each adapted to its particular context, have been established in the past twenty years in places such as Argentina, Chile, Timor-Leste, El Salvador, and Guatemala. Their overall record of success is uneven. But reading Bishop Tutu's account, one thinks of the potential for similar commissions in Iraq or Afghanistan when the time is right—especially if they can be set up by the stakeholders themselves and not imposed from without.

Much diplomacy in the past century has been based in a paradigm of the military iron fist inside the velvet glove of negotiation, as nations have jockeyed for the power they were certain was necessary to their security. William Ury, the author of *The Third Side* and other books about conflict, offers an alternative that goes beyond this "us-and-them" conception of power. Ury's term "the third side" refers to the idea that although conflict is usually viewed as two-sided ("you're either with us or against us"), conflict resolution requires a "third side" that is not advocating for either combatant, but instead advocates for resolution. Ury reports that in some tribal societies where maintenance of positive relations is seen as critical to survival, when two members of the clan become engaged in a dispute, the rest of the clan, instead of choosing sides, promotes the resolution of the dispute. Significantly, the third side even includes relatives of the combatants.

Ury writes about the immense potential of nonviolent conflict resolution:

> Conflict today poses the same challenge that fire once did. Before the twentieth century, fire was one of people's greatest fears. In a few minutes, a fire raging out of control could destroy everything—houses, crops, fields and lives. Cities, with their closely placed buildings, posed the worst danger. When Mrs. O'Leary's cow kicked over a lantern in 1871, it began a fire that consumed most of Chicago. Yet, for all its evident danger, fire was long regarded as a natural and inevitable tragedy, part of human fate.
>
> That is no longer true today in modern cities. Thanks to building regulations and fireproof materials, emergency

exits and smoke detectors, and fire fighters and trucks—in short, a comprehensive fire-prevention system—urban dwellers live largely free of fear of fire.

We have an analogous opportunity today when it comes to preventing destructive conflict. We can give up our belief in its inevitability, and learn step by step how to prevent, resolve and contain it. Our challenge is to create such systems in every social domain—from our families to our organizations, from our neighborhoods to our nations, and from our interpersonal relationships to our world.

If we prove successful, schoolchildren may wonder one day why serious conflicts ever escalated into wars. They may be astonished why people did not take the simple steps necessary to prevent conflagration. They may puzzle over why people did not see that whatever an effective system might cost in time or effort, its price was but a pittance compared to the exorbitant cost of destructive conflict.[4]

One of the conflicts on the planet that seems most intractable is that between Israelis and Palestinians. Each of these factions tells itself and the world a complex story that justifies its use of violence. For the Jews, hundreds of years of oppression in Europe and elsewhere, followed by the Nazis' systematic attempt to wipe them off the face of the earth, rationalized the forceful establishment of a homeland where they could find safe haven. Inevitably, Palestinians occupying the same contested space perceive its confiscation, however well intentioned or necessary from the Jewish frame of reference, as deeply and everlastingly unfair.

If there is any region on earth where a third world war might begin, it would be today's Middle East. Israel is said to possess a substantial nuclear arsenal. Elements of the Iranian government apparently want these weapons as equalizers of the balance of power. We all share a vital interest in resolving the Israeli-Palestinian conflict nonviolently. The words of the old labor song ask, "Which side are you on?" The answer must be Ury's *third side*. Every member of the human clan anywhere who stands up for nonviolent resolution helps to create an environment that is safer not only for Israelis or Palestinians but for all of us.

Fortunately, there are positive initiatives being taken that, like Clint Eastwood's two movies about Iwo Jima, attempt to bring together separate narratives that seem unalterably opposed. For example, the Peace Research Institute in the Middle East is using a series of workbooks to help students understand the histories of both sides and expand their awareness of the "other."[5]

Some students in the Middle East are not waiting for such academic reframing of parallel stories but are beginning to use means like the Internet's Facebook to reach out directly to one another, refusing to be enemies and instead establishing relationships of common understanding and reconciliation.[6] Chapter 10 outlines the process of dialogue through which people can participate in this deep sharing of one another's narratives.

THE CONTRIBUTION OF APPROPRIATE HUMANITARIAN FOREIGN AID TO DEVELOPING COUNTRIES

A second strategy that is far better than war is the contribution of appropriate foreign aid to developing countries. The United States and other industrialized nations agreed to give 0.7 percent of their GDP (Gross Domestic Product) each year as foreign aid. Currently, the United States gives 0.17 percent, far below the agreed-upon goal, and half of that goes to Israel and Egypt. While the actual dollar amount given is large, because the U.S. GDP is so large, we are not meeting our commitments. Sweden, Holland, and Denmark, on the other hand, are giving 1 percent or more.[7] In 2006, people in the U.S. spent almost twice as much on pet food as their government did on foreign aid. Helping others in the developing world pull themselves up by their boot-straps means less hunger, less unemployment, less desperation, less resentment. This fosters friendship and increases goodwill and respect for America; so it is clearly in our self-interest. When people's basic needs are met, there is less hopelessness and anger, and that decreases the appeal of terrorism as a strategy. There are many models and examples of foreign aid projects, by both governments and private organizations, that meet real human needs and provide value far beyond their cost.

One of the most familiar is the U.S. Peace Corps. Corps volunteers help villagers around the world grow crops, start cottage industries, and improve community health and infrastructure.

The Peace Corps began in 1960 when then-Senator John F. Kennedy challenged college students to serve their nation by working in developing countries. Since then, more than 178,000 volunteers have helped in 138 countries.

Three simple goals comprise the Peace Corps' mission:

1. helping the people of interested countries in meeting their needs for trained men and women
2. helping promote a better understanding of Americans on the part of the peoples served
3. helping promote a better understanding of other peoples on the part of all Americans.[8]

Rotary International provides another example of a constructive humanitarian initiative. One of the organization's tenets is to foster international goodwill. Rotary's sponsorship of the Peace Trees Vietnam project is helping rid that country of landmines one field at a time, so that productive farmland can be reclaimed.[9]

Giving aid to large groups of impoverished people doesn't have to be expensive, as Greg Mortenson's Central Asia Institute proves.[10] After a failed climb in the Himalayas on K2, Greg stumbled into a village, frostbitten and weak, and the people nursed him back to health. He vowed to repay them.

In the last twelve years, in cooperation with local villagers,

Greg has been instrumental in building over seventy-four schools, which have educated 15,000 children in remote areas of Pakistan along the Afghani-Pakistan border. In communities with those schools, 95 percent of parents chose to send their children to Greg's schools rather than the local anti-Western fundamentalist schools operated by the Taliban.

Greg finds competent teachers, whom he pays $20 a month, the going rate there. Compare this to making indiscriminate war upon areas where people feel enmity toward the United States and where villagers protect the al-Qaeda network. The Taliban have left Greg's projects alone, because villagers have bought into the idea of the schools.[11] Greg is addressing terrorism with goodwill and books, not bombs. For the cost of a single Predator unmanned aircraft,[12] Greg could serve far more than 15,000 students, because he could afford to pay 15,000 *teachers*—for ten years!

Greg Mortenson's initiatives have an indigenous historical precedent. In Afghanistan in the 1930s, a follower of Gandhi named Abdul Ghaffar Khan put together a nonviolent army of Pashtun tribesmen who also built schools in the region.[13] The army was viciously attacked by British colonial forces but refused to respond in kind. Ghaffar Khan's story helps to dissolve the stereotype in the West that automatically equates Islam with violence.

The dedicated men and women of the armed forces of the United States, given the need and the opportunity, have generated lasting good feeling in people they have helped in their response to tragedies such as the Sumatran tsunami and the typhoon that hit Bangladesh in November of 2007. After the devastating earthquake that shook the Mansehra region of northern Pakistan in October 2005, American helicopters were quickly dispatched to help with rescue and to distribute food, tents, and medical supplies in an area not known for pro-U.S. sentiments. The good impression left by this relief effort made lasting changes in local opinion.[14]

As Paul Hawken reports in his book on NGOs, *Blessed Unrest,* there are literally millions of other examples of initiatives that allow us to obtain enormous returns in goodwill and friendships for very little investment.

RESPECT FOR AND ADHERENCE TO INTERNATIONAL LAW

Our goals are those of the U.N.'s founders who sought to replace a world at war with one where the rule of law would prevail . . . where conflict would give way to freedom from violence.

—Ronald Reagan[15]

A third strategy to resolve conflict and prevent war is to respect and adhere to international law. The International Criminal Court in The Hague, Netherlands, tries individuals for crimes against humanity. The United States is not among the 139 nations that have joined. If we really want terrorists brought to justice, we have to be willing to participate in an impartial international legal system. Instead, the United States chose to set up its Guantanamo prison for terrorist suspects, an institution that is so far outside accepted legal norms that it may end up becoming completely ineffective.

The International Court of Justice is a branch of the United Nations that prosecutes countries for crimes against humanity. The United States has resigned from the court, fearing that the possible prosecution of its leaders or soldiers would compromise its sovereignty. But when all nations in the world agree to abide by a set of rules that apply fairly and equally, we will all be more secure.

Lawyers and U.N. representatives still debate whether the U.S. invasion of Iraq in 2002 was a violation of international law. The U.N. Security Council did authorize the application of military force to end the occupation of Kuwait by Saddam Hussein. The ceasefire of that war in 1991 was conditional on Iraqi disarmament. So Iraq's failure to disarm could be said to revive the authorization to use force.[16] The invasion of Iraq by coalition forces in the second Gulf War points up the conflict between an obsolete paradigm of lawless force in international affairs and a new paradigm of adherence to international law that has been slowly taking shape since the two world wars. It is a step in the right direction that nations at least consider their actions in the context of an international framework of law, even as they continue to rationalize those actions according to archaic notions of self-interest.

The precedent of the preemptive use of force set by the second Gulf War may come back to haunt not only the United States but the whole international community. The dialogue about sovereignty is an incentive for nations to clarify how better to act in legal concert against potential security threats. Sovereignty on a small, interconnected planet remains a difficult issue. How should the world respond to repressive regimes such as that of Myanmar, which refused to open its borders to international aid after a typhoon submerged much of the country, or that of Sudan,[17] which exacerbates the horrors of Darfur? Sovereignty has been an especially important principle for the United States, but preemptive war directly violates the sovereignty of the nation attacked. Inevitably, the world community will perceive unilateral attacks on other nations that also value their sovereignty as only another example of "might makes right," the old double standard that is the opposite of the Golden Rule. Meanwhile, ironically, the sovereignty of the United States has been not so subtly undermined by our accumulation of such enormous debt to other countries.

COOPERATION AND COLLABORATION
WITH OTHER NATIONS

To counter unilateralism, a fourth way we can help prevent war and resolve conflicts worldwide is through cooperation and collaboration. For centuries, nations have cooperated in uneasy alliances against perceived adversaries. Now we must learn to cooperate on the basis of the obsolescence of war, the interdependence of all people, and the consistency of ends and means. Just as war has become obsolete, so has any nation's "national interest" when it is perceived to be different from that of the whole Earth. Americans have a long history of working with other peoples and countries around the world as a collaborative partner to help solve global problems, such as the eradication of smallpox and polio, feeding the hungry, and protecting endangered species. Other nations have rallied to work with us, and the results have benefited us all.

In this endeavor the United Nations has been and will continue to be indispensable. The United Nations is one of our best hopes; all countries should cooperate to help it overcome its shortcomings and fulfill its mission. If a part of our own national judicial system or police force or Congress became corrupt, we wouldn't scrap it. We would try to fix it. The United Nations' present structure, based on conditions when it was founded just after the end of World War II, badly needs an overhaul to reflect present challenges faced by the world community. More than ever, it will become a locus where nations pursue dialogue with one another across perceived cultural divides about common goals. The planet will have an increasing need for well-trained U.N.-mandated peacekeeping forces that can deploy rapidly to prevent future conflicts from escalating.

The core values of the United Nations are the rule of law, the protection of civilians, mutual respect between people of different faiths and cultures, and the peaceful resolution of conflicts. These excerpts from the U.N. Charter show that its mission is even more important today:

> To save succeeding generations from the scourge of war . . .
> To unite our strength to maintain international peace and security . . .[18]

In the 1990s alone, U.N. peacekeepers helped to prevent, diffuse, or resolve over thirty-five conflicts around the world, in such places as East Timor, Haiti, Cambodia, Somalia, Sierra Leone, and Kosovo.

U.N. Under-Secretary General Shashi Tharoor argues that the United Nations, far from being irrelevant, continues to be indispensable:

> The second half of the 20th century, though far from perfect, was a spectacular improvement on the first half, for one simple reason: because, in and after 1945, a group of far-sighted leaders drew up rules to govern international behavior, founding institutions in which different nations could cooperate, under universally applicable rules, for the common good.
>
> . . . President Harry Truman put it clearly to the assembled signatories of the U.N. charter in San Francisco on 26 June 1945: "You have created a great instrument for peace and security and human progress in the world . . . if we fail to use it, we shall betray all those who have died in order that we might meet here in freedom and safety to create it. If we seek to use it selfishly—for the advantage of any one nation or any small group of nations—we shall be equally guilty of that betrayal . . . We all have to recognize, no matter how great our strength, that we must deny ourselves the license to do always as we please. No one nation . . . can or should expect any special privilege which harms any other nation . . . Unless we are all willing to pay that price, no organization for world peace can accomplish its purpose. And what a reasonable price that is!"
>
> . . . No, the Security Council is not perfect. It has acted unwisely at times, and failed to act at others . . . Even so, the U.N.'s record of success is better than many national institutions. As Dag Hammarskjold, the great second

Secretary-General put it, the U.N. was not created to take humanity to heaven, but to save it from hell.

And that it has done, innumerable times. During the Cold War the U.N. played the indispensable role of preventing regional crises and conflicts from igniting a superpower conflagration. Its peacekeeping operations make the difference between life and death for millions around the world . . . there's nothing else like it.[19]

We live in an increasingly interconnected world. The largest challenges facing us are transnational, ones that Einstein couldn't even imagine when he looked ahead and spoke of the fundamental change that would come with nuclear weapons—challenges like terrorism, ocean pollution, coral-reef death, and cross-border epidemics. We cannot solve global problems alone. If we want other countries to help us with these issues, we have to be willing to participate in international treaties and agreements that benefit everyone.

Unfortunately, the list of the collaborative treaties that the United States rejects as of 2008 is extensive: the Comprehensive Nuclear Test Ban Treaty, the Anti-Ballistic Missile Treaty (the cornerstone of arms control for thirty years, which the United States signed initially, but withdrew from in 2001); treaties to ban the international sale of small arms, land mines, biological and chemical weapons, and cluster bombs; treaties that protect the rights of women and children; and treaties to control the rate of global CO_2 emissions. By participating in these treaties to which the vast majority of nations have become signatories, the United States could help make the world, as well as itself, healthier and safer.

One of the most significant areas of collaboration concerns the reduction and elimination of nuclear arms. South Africa gave up nuclear weapons, as did Ukraine, Kazakhstan, and Belarus after they inherited them from the breakup of the Soviet Union. Libya gave up its attempt to develop nuclear weapons. Writing in the *Wall Street Journal* on January 4, 2007, a quartet of establishment voices, Henry Kissinger, George Shultz, Sam Nunn, and William Perry, called for the total elimination of these weapons.[20] The writers of that remarkable editorial are not exactly unworldly dreamers. Dr. Kissinger was secretary of state from 1973 to 1977. Mr. Shultz, a distinguished fellow at the Hoover Institution at Stanford, was secretary of state from 1982 to 1989. Mr. Perry was secretary of defense from 1994 to 1997. Mr. Nunn is former chairman of the Senate Armed Services Committee.

Of course, even if a nuclear-free world becomes a reality, the warheads can always be reconstituted. This stubborn fact underscores the profundity of our challenge: it is necessary but not sufficient to abolish the weapons, which are only a symptom of the way we think.

But seeing establishment figures come forward with these proposals for nuclear abolition nourishes hope. For such proposals to become the acting policy of governments, large numbers of individual citizens must agree about them and advocate for their usefulness. How can that happen? What exactly is the work that has to be done? The final section outlines the large-scale educational process that must take place in the United States and worldwide in order for new agreements about nuclear weapons and the obsolescence of war to bear fruit in concrete changes of policy.

QUESTIONS FOR DIALOGUE

1. Why is the United States so reluctant to participate in treaties and agreements that almost every other country in the world has signed? Is this approach working for us? If not, why? If so, why?
2. Where does most of the foreign aid given by the United States go? What changes in priorities, if any, would you make in these disbursements?
3. What do you think is the value of the United Nations? How would you define its problems? If you were in a position to change the structure of the United Nations for the greater good, not of any one country but for all countries, what would you do?

4. Discuss the concept of national sovereignty in an interdependent world. What are some alternatives open to the world community when a country refuses humanitarian aid to its own people?
5. What does it mean to negotiate nuclear weapons down to zero, given that they can be rebuilt? Even if the proposals of Kissinger, Shultz, Perry, and Nunn are welcome and necessary, are they sufficient? If not, what else needs to happen to increase global safety and security?
6. What are some of the problems that international cooperation and collaboration have already solved? What should the next priorities for cooperation between nations be?

NOTES

1. Douglas P Fry, *Beyond War: The Human Potential for Peace* (New York: Oxford University Press, 2007), xiv.
2. See Njabulo Ndebele's commencement speech in appendix D, p. 172.
3. Bishop Tutu is quoted in Michael Collopy, *Architects of Peace: Visions of Hope in Words and Images* (Novato, CA: New World Library, 2002), 115.
4. William Ury, *The Third Side* (New York: Penguin, 2000), 169.
5. Israeli-Palestinian Workbook Initiative, http://traubman.igc.org/textbooknight.htm.
6. http://soliya.net; http://mepeace.org.
7. The budgeting process of the U.S. government makes it extremely difficult to compile exact current figures for the distribution of foreign aid, and especially to discern how much is disbursed in the form of weapons and how much for nonmilitary projects; see Anup Shah, "US and Foreign Aid Assistance," http://www.globalissues.org/Trade Related/Debt/USAid.asp.
8. www.peacecorps.gov.
9. http://www.peacetreesvietnam.org/the-team.htm.
10. https://www.ikat.org/. See also Gregg Mortenson, *Three Cups of Tea: One Man's Mission to Fight Terrorism and Build Nations—One School at a Time* (New York: Viking, 2006).
11. Nicholas D. Kristoff, "It Takes a School, Not Missiles," http://

www.nytimes.com/2008/07/13/opinion/13kristof.html?ex=12166128 00&en=c5d9a9ad6353b482&ei=5070&emc=eta1.

12. The cost of a single Predator unmanned aircraft is $3.5 million; http://www.globalsecurity.org/military/library/budget/fy1999/dot-e/ airforce/99predator.html. (The Pentagon has ordered 3,000 copies of Greg's book.)

13. See "Pashtun Pacifists," *Timeline* (publication of the Foundation for Global Community), May/June 2002, 6-7.

14. *New York Times*, October 26, 2005.

15. Address before the 38th Session of the U.N. General Assembly; www.reagan.utexas.edu/archives/speeches/1983/92683a.htm.

16. See appendix B, p. 166, for a British law professor's perspective on the issues of international law relevant to the second Gulf War.

17. In July of 2008, the International Criminal Court indicted the president and vice-president of Sudan on charges of genocide and crimes against humanity, the first time a sitting head of state has been charged by the court.

18. http://www.un.org/aboutun/charter/.

19. Shashi Tharoor, *The New Internationalist* 375 (Jan/Feb 2005).

20. *Wall Street Journal*, January 4, 2007. An abbreviated text of the editorial can be found below in appendix C, p. 168.

PART FOUR

THE CHALLENGE OF CHANGE

There are some things only governments can do, such as negotiating binding agreements. But there are some things that only citizens outside government can do, such as changing human relationships.
— Dr. Harold Saunders, former U.S. assistant secretary
of state and negotiator of the Camp David Accords
(http://traubman.igc.org/messages/451.htm)

8

The Process of Change

Public sentiment is everything. With public sentiment nothing can fail; without it, nothing can succeed. Consequently, he who molds public sentiment goes deeper than he who enacts statutes or pronounces decisions. He makes statutes or decisions possible or impossible to be executed.

—Abraham Lincoln[1]

BUILDING AGREEMENT ON PRINCIPLE

 A seamless web of connection ties together the personal and the international. The collective psyche of a nation is the aggregate of millions of individual minds. Nations cannot "think" in a new way about violence or move beyond "us-and-them" conceptions of global security unless individuals commit to new thinking and acting in their personal lives.

In a democracy, elected officials cannot get too far in front of the people. The people must lead the leaders. Therefore, the goal is to get to a place where enough citizens understand that war is obsolete, that we are one on this planet, and that the means are the ends in the making. Our task is to build widespread agreement about the truth and practical utility of these principles and their personal and policy implications. It is the great work of our time to seed these principles into both our private lives and public discourse. It is not political work in the sense of one party seeking competitive advantage, because it seeks to build agreement among all parties.

Along with our unwillingness to examine our own role in the systemic drift toward war and violence, another feature of the American character is a narrow definition of what constitutes effective action. We often assume talk will get us only so far unless it is followed by action that leads directly to concrete results. This view is understandable. The challenge of ending war is so big and so urgent that people feel compelled to accomplish something tangible and measurable.

Are educating and building agreement action? Absolutely. Not only are they action, they are the necessary actions, because agreement or consensus must precede any effective legislation. Agreement is a necessary foundation for law because, without agreement, law is unenforceable.

Prohibition is a useful example. In 1920, this nation amended the Constitution—the most tangible result one could ask for—to prohibit the manufacture, sale, and transportation of alcoholic beverages. But people flouted the law; the illicit liquor business thrived. Why? Agreement did not exist among citizens that alcohol should be outlawed. Prohibition was repealed only a decade later. In the same way, even a constitutional amendment banning war would be but a brief "noble experiment" that would fail if agreement were not built first.

Our understanding of the fundamental founding principle of the United States, that "all men are created equal," is an excellent example of the process of social change and building agreement. In 1776, our society's agreement on this principle could best be stated as "all white, property-owning males are created equal." Laws restricting voting and allowing slavery reflected this agreement. Later, as our society measured itself against the meaning of "all men are created equal," we were confronted by the brutal fact of a system that traded in human beings.

Slavery was accepted and considered normal, woven tightly into the web of the economies of nations. The right to hold slaves was accepted by all major religions and by virtually every government around the planet. The process of ending institutionalized slavery took the better part of two centuries.

At the time of the American Revolution, new notions of human rights and freedoms provided an important moral framework for the antislavery movement—slavery as utterly inconsistent with basic rights. Over a period of years, however, as the principles of the Revolution became more distant, this inconsistency was rationalized. The deeply rooted slavery system in the South was strongly defended during the 1800s as the cotton economy developed.

What had begun as a staunch nonviolent movement found increasing numbers of abolitionists in the 1850s resorting to violence. The opportunity to continue a process of reform was slowed by reactions to these extremist approaches. Dialogue became nonexistent, and political lines were drawn that led to the Civil War. But the growing conviction that slavery was wrong sustained the nation through the bloodiest, most costly conflict in American history. That same conviction on the part of many people in Europe prevented England and France from coming to the aid of the Confederacy.

The movement to end slavery began with individuals, few in number, *deciding* to address the basic moral and ethical rights of human beings.

> By the early 1770s . . . in Britain, France and the North American colonies there were forces in motion that would lead to organized movements to abolish the African trade and the entire institutional framework which permitted human beings to be treated as things. Although slavery was almost as old as human history, this was something new in the world . . . On one side were the classical and Christian theories of servitude which tended to rationalize the brute fact that forced labor had been an integral part of the American experience. On the other side were

increasing strains in the traditional system of values, *the emergence of new modes of thought and feeling*, and a growing faith in the possibility of moral progress which was to some extent associated with the symbolic meaning of the New World. But in the last analysis, such trends and contexts and backgrounds are only abstractions. No matter how "ripe" the time, there would be no coalescing of antislavery opinion until *specific decisions and commitments were taken by individual people.* [emphasis added][2]

These individuals included former slaves such as Frederick Douglass, who worked tirelessly on the issue of abolition, and William Wilberforce, a British Quaker whose efforts to pass an antislavery bill in Parliament persisted for decades. At first, most people could not see the possibility of a world without slavery. There were seemingly insurmountable economic, political, and human problems to overcome. As the few who saw the possibility and the necessity worked to spread the idea, the impossible happened. Agreement grew and implementation followed. Slavery was abolished.

With the emancipation of the slaves, we in the United States gained further understanding of "all men are created equal." In time, we instituted women's suffrage and civil rights. The best expression of our current understanding of this founding principle is, "all U.S. citizens are created equal."

The next natural step would take this principle to its highest form of expression: "All people in the world are created equal." This complements the Latin motto of our nation, *e pluribus unum,* "out of many, one." We are many individuals, communities, races, and religions in the United States of America. At the same time, our nation is only one among many who must learn to live together on one planet, equally dependent on one life-support system. The collective destinies of the nations of the world are absolutely interrelated. We must build agreement that if a principle is true, it must apply to all who share this world with us.

But it is self-contradictory to impose such guiding principles by force. Building agreement about a world beyond war is a two-step process. First, we need to build agreement that war doesn't work; it is counterproductive against terrorism, its costs are unacceptable, and it could lead to unprecedented global destruction. Second, we need to agree about better alternatives. People fully support decisions only if they have played a part in the decision-making process. The outcome will be stronger for having had the benefit of many different viewpoints. Until agreement is reached, laws are premature. Only when we have agreement can effective implementation occur.

THE DIFFUSION OF INNOVATIONS

Others are affected by what I am, and say, and do. And these others have also their sphere of influence. So that a single act of mine may spread in widening circles through a nation or humanity.

—William Ellery Channing[3]

How much agreement is "enough"? Everett Rogers, a professor at Stanford University, studied the diffusion of innovations through society.[4] Whether it was ideas or brand names or the demand for hybrid cars, he found that the general pattern of initial skepticism and gradual acceptance could be graphed by an S-shaped curve that gradually steepens and then levels off.

The good news is that Rogers asserted that if only 5 percent of the population takes up an innovation, it becomes what he called "embedded," which means that the idea is here to stay. Even if not immediately adopted by the majority, it will continue to be developed and refined by innovators. Rogers asserted that ten times that number, 50 percent, must become *aware* of the new idea for 5 percent actually to adopt it.

Rogers went on to posit that if only one-fifth of people, 20

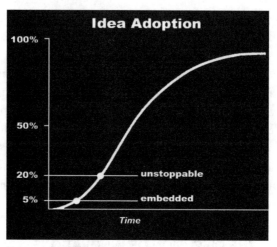

Figure 2. Rogers Graph of Idea Adoption

percent, actually *adopt* the idea, it becomes unstoppable. In the lead-up to the Revolutionary War, for example, only about 20 percent of the American colonists were in favor of independence. But that turned out to be enough.

After the 20 percent level is reached, the diffusion and adoption of the idea then continues almost automatically up the curve. Much work is still required, but at that stage the work consists of implementation, rather than simply trying to convince people that the idea is worthy of consideration. It is possible that we may be approaching, or even be beyond, an "unstoppable" level of agreement with former Vice-President Al Gore that only a pervasive and deep response to global climate change, affecting all our institutions, will be sufficient to sustain the planet.

At first the idea or product feels so new that only a very few people are willing to adopt it. Because the idea is still seen as utopian or far-fetched, the recognized leaders of society are rarely among this group. The innovation is considered too different from the existing beliefs and values of society.

In this first phase of the curve, proponents of a new idea must work incessantly just to keep the idea alive. Work at this stage is often frustrating and seems not to be additive. But that is only an illusion. People courageous enough to adopt new ideas are laying the foundation for a structure that may not be completed in their lifetimes. Others will build on that foundation.

With time, as innovators communicate the idea, it begins to gain social acceptability. A somewhat larger group, which Rogers called the "early adopters," now including recognized leaders, takes up the innovation. The rest of society Rogers divided into two still larger groups and one somewhat smaller one: the "early majority," "late majority," and the "late adopters," or traditionalists. Traditionalists, motivated by skepticism and caution, generally come around to a new idea only when they are sure it is safe, effective, "tried and true."

The gradual change in opinions and values that led to the abolition of slavery conformed to this S-shaped curve. But the curve operates identically in the acceptance of less profound innovations. For example, people were at first cautious about the technology of hybrid cars. Were the batteries reliable? As time passed and gas prices continued to mount, the growing attractiveness of hybrids helped to accelerate demand, and we began to see them everywhere, reassuring larger and larger groups of people that hybrid cars were as safe and dependable as conventional combustion-engine automobiles. While not everyone may end up buying a hybrid, no one raises a skeptical eyebrow any longer at what at first seemed a radical experiment in transportation.

Understanding this process of social change explains how the supposedly impossible becomes possible. As more and more people adopt the new idea, the cultural environment changes. What was radical becomes avant-garde; what was avant-garde becomes a commonly accepted understanding.

Throughout the process, it is crucial to differentiate between momentary events and deep structural change. Change on the surface may masquerade as more fundamental progress. Just as the Vietnam War finally ended, so, eventually, will the Iraq war. Or perhaps we will read that some nation's nuclear program is not as advanced as we thought, and breathe a sigh of relief. But the underlying trends will remain, trends that call the human species to forge a new set of agreements that leave war behind. Even if the planet rids itself of every nuclear weapon, it is impossible for our species to forget how to make them. They are only a symptom of the way we think. The change in thinking demanded of us is far deeper than successful nuclear disarmament.

The Rogers graph (figure 2) is hopeful not only in its percentages but because of what it tells us about how to be most efficient in our outreach and educational focus. If we count ourselves among the "innovators" or "early adopters," we have the best shot at accelerating adoption of the principles by seeking out other innovators or early adopters. They are the ones who are most likely to be open to hearing a new idea from us. According to Rogers's thinking, we may be wasting valuable time and energy to try to convince "traditionalists," who are waiting cautiously for a given innovation to prove its worth.

Nevertheless, if we are skilled at opening dialogue, we can never tell who might respond. One might make the assumption that veterans who have endured actual combat would be traditionalists when it comes to the value of war. Instead, there are hundreds of chapters of organizations such as Veterans for Peace and Winter Soldiers, people who have endured the realities of combat in Vietnam or Iraq and who would do anything to prevent others from having to go through the horrors they experienced. They have seen up close the futility and obsolescence of war.

Motivated by what Gandhi called "truth-force," we can seek the support of others who share our convictions and our desire to learn. This will give us the experience and courage to take our concerns before a larger public. There are as many ways to spread a new idea as there are businesses, places of worship, schools, media, and every other site of potential dialogue.

Around the world, millions of people in nongovernmental organizations are exploring everything from how to help impoverished African countries join the world economy to putting the brakes on the sale of small arms. The sociologist Paul Ray has suggested that there are many more people than we might assume who think of themselves as what he calls "cultural creatives."[5] These are people who are open to change both in themselves and in the world, and open also to greater involvement and activism—if they can both find one another and become convinced that their efforts would be genuinely cumulative. Tools like the Internet are making new webs of connection not only possible but surprisingly rapid, as we have seen in the sophisticated use of the Net made by political campaigns in the United States.

The consolidation of the will to end war is occurring. In the United States, since 1985, eight national organizations including the United States Institute of Peace have articulated the goal of ending war. Several churches have proclaimed the objective. One hundred and two third-world nations stated the legitimacy of the goal in 1988. These institutions do not speak for wistful peaceniks. They speak for serious, thoughtful people who see no other recourse that can enable a meaningful step forward in human development.

—Col. John Barr, USMC (ret.)

The success of the women's movement and the civil rights movement in bringing about a change in thinking was dependent on a few dedicated people who chose to live their lives in alignment with a new idea. The first step is always a decision to say yes to the idea and commit to live one's life as if it were already a reality, in the spirit of Gandhi's exhortation to "be the change you want to see in the world." People who rise to the challenge of living beyond war are like hybrid cars: they are an advertisement for the attractiveness and practicality of something new. The next step is to find other like-minded people and invite them to make the same decision. The third step is to find effective means to project this idea into the culture in a way that is consistent with the idea itself.

These steps hardly represent a linear progression toward utopia. They only begin a lifetime journey. When we encounter ill will or unconsciousness in ourselves, we become open to learning what we need to do to get back on track. Over and over for the rest of our lives we will travel this path of experiencing nonalignment, figuring out why we are out of alignment, and shifting back into alignment. As we do this, we will get better at it, and nonalignment will perhaps come up less frequently, though the need for self-aware vigilance will never disappear. But because we are at least a little more integrated as time passes, our lives will speak more clearly to others of the change that is needed and the real possibility that it can occur.

Connecting with other people of similar intention, we will get valuable feedback from them, and we will educate one another to become clearer and more authentic examples of the change that is needed. As our numbers grow, our collective example will have more and more influence and the S-curve of agreement will gradually steepen. As we project the idea into the culture, the culture itself will feed back to us new information that will enable us to project our ideas more effectively.

The seat of all resistance to change and the root cause of war are our own individual egos, our sense of ourselves as separate. If we stay on the path of dropping our "us-and-them" thinking and realigning ourselves with the goodwill that we recognize in ourselves and actively seek out in others, then our institutions and the people in charge of them will be compelled to address the reality that war is obsolete, that we are all in this together, and that the means are the ends in the making. This outcome is dependent on our being true to our beliefs throughout the process—on our "walking our talk." We know it is possible to live beyond war. The question is, will we decide to do it?

Never doubt that a small group of thoughtful, committed citizens can change the world. Indeed, it is the only thing that ever has.

—Margaret Mead[6]

QUESTIONS FOR DIALOGUE

1. Did Everett Rogers's S-curve change your thinking about the possibility of making a difference? If so, how?
2. Inventory your circle of family, friends, and colleagues. With whom would you be able to have a dialogue about moving beyond war?

NOTES

1. Abraham Lincoln, first debate with Stephen Douglas, in *Abraham Lincoln: Speeches and Writings 1832-1858,* ed. Don E. Fehrenbacher (New York: Library of America, 2009), 524-25.

2. David Bryan Davis, *The Problem of Slavery in Western Culture* (New York: Oxford University Press, 1988), 489.

3. http://biblegems.blogspot.com/2008/02/gems-from-february-2008.html.

4. See Everett Rogers, The Stanford Research Institute, http://www.sri.com/; and Everett Rogers, *Diffusion of Innovations*, 3rd ed. (New York: Free Press, 1983).

5. Paul Ray and Sherry Ruth Anderson, *Cultural Creatives: How 50 Million People Are Changing the World,* (New York: Three Rivers Press, 2001).

6. http://www.quotationspage.com/quote/33522.html.

9
Decision

To put an end to outward war, you must begin to put an end to war in yourself. Some of you will nod your heads and say, "I agree," and go outside and do exactly the same as you have been doing for the last ten or twenty years. Your agreement is merely verbal and has no significance, for the world's miseries and wars are not going to be stopped by your casual assent. They will be stopped only when you realize the danger, when you realize your responsibility, when you do not leave it to somebody else. If you realize the suffering, if you see the urgency of immediate action and do not postpone, then you will transform yourself; peace will come only when you yourself are peaceful, when you yourself are at peace with your neighbor.

—Jiddu Krishnamurti, philosopher[1]

Knowing that war is obsolete and that better alternatives are available is one thing. Personally deciding to reject war and violence forever as an option is quite another. We know we can live beyond war. Will we? When confronted with such a dilemma, there is a natural tendency to postpone making a decision, to drift. We avoid facing the issue squarely. Perhaps we assume that a trip to the voting booth every four years is enough. We project unrealistic, godlike powers onto our elected officials, subconsciously hoping that a "great leader" will solve the problem for us. And often our leaders disappoint us, because *their* decision making is constrained by the "us-and-them" mind-set of their constituency—both civic and corporate. We maintain the illusory hope that people will realize how insane it would be to slip into a nuclear exchange, along with the complementary illusion that it is too big for us to do anything about. Or we simply put the issue out of our minds, hoping it will magically disappear. We resist the reality of this unprecedented threat to our well-being, and we do not take responsibility for the critical role we each must play. A clear-cut personal decision is needed to pierce through the gray fog of indecision into the light.

Deciding to venture into the unknown, so critical to the change required in our thinking about war, is not alien to us as individuals or as members of society. We have all made decisions that have influenced the course of our lives without knowing the full implications: whether or not to pursue a college education; the choice of an occupation; moving to a new city; getting married or staying single; whether or not to have children. By their nature, all these critical decisions are made without knowing the full implications. Indeed, we often know very little.

A true decision must be total. Unless we totally reject war as an obsolete, unworkable, and ultimately fatal approach, we will not discover how to move, and to live, beyond war. A decision is powerful. Anyone who has succeeded, for example, in quitting smoking knows the power and finality of a decision. Decision means to cut ("cision") away from ("de")—to enter into the unknown by rejecting and forever closing the door to an existing option. Deciding to move beyond war consists of a no and a yes: no to war, and yes to building a world beyond war. Until we decide to reject war and violence as viable solutions, we will not be able to fully join with those who have already said yes to all the possibilities that lie beyond war.

We are already aware of many of these possibilities. We can see them in the community of Neve Shalom Wahat al Salam, in the Israeli and Palestinian soldiers who have decided to work together for understanding rather than to justify killing one another, or the growing list of millions of nongovernmental organizations worldwide that are working in the trenches of peace-building and sustainability. But even if we are not part of an NGO, to put a copy of those foundational principles and core practices on our refrigerator door and begin to let their light affect our daily activities is a significant and valuable step into a new world.

Why us and why now? Because the agent of change over whom we have the most control is ourselves. Much as we might wish to place blame on others or hope that experts and leaders will solve our collective challenges, there is no way around personal responsibility. Simply by being alive, we use resources, produce waste, and make a difference in terms of our attitude and what we do—or don't do. There is no way for us *not* to make a difference. Therefore, we cannot avoid deciding the kind of difference we want to make. Our current crisis is the result of individuals making the wrong kind of difference: either doing nothing or acting on the basis of obsolete ways of thinking. In all societal changes—abolishing slavery, instituting women's suffrage, advancing civil rights—it has been individual people who have made the crucial difference. That is the only way it works. It works because individuals do not ask, "Can I really make a difference?" They ask, "What must I do?" Upon finding the answer, they do it.

While this decision may occur at one point in time, it is a lifelong process to learn to live our lives consistently. It is not easy to change the way we think and act. The core practices of resolving conflict, maintaining goodwill, and working together, far from promising instant perfection, put us on a lifetime path of discovery, learning from our mistakes and from one another. While we may hold a life beyond war as a personal ideal, we must accept our human fallibility, pick ourselves up when we err, and put ourselves back on the path with renewed determination. In deciding to work together, we can give one another consent to provide and receive honest feedback and to resolve, rather than brush under the rug, the uncomfortable conflicts that are an inevitable component of human relations. I'll help you learn to do this if you'll help me.

This training results in a new kind of intelligence, without which intelligence as it is usually measured, intellectual cleverness or competitively advancing one's own interest at the expense of the whole, remains dangerously incomplete. To meet our challenges creatively, we need one another in our fullest presence, authenticity, and inclusiveness. This does not mean we become instantly perfect or that we have to. To be human is to be forever growing, learning, and evolving.

We each must be living proof that a world beyond war is possible. Individuals are the units of social change. Without individuals making a decision to change, societal change cannot occur. It is only through grounding ourselves in principles that work in our own lives that we can create a grassroots precedent from which large-scale collective change will follow. Experiencing the practical reward of watching these implications work in ourselves and those closest to us can give us confidence that the same principles and personal practices will work on the world stage. In this process, one of the most powerful tools for engaging others to feel a similar confidence is dialogue.

We can't solve problems by using the same kind of thinking that we used when we created them.

—Albert Einstein[2]

QUESTIONS FOR DIALOGUE

1. Think of an important decision in your life. How did you decide? How much did you know in advance about the outcome?
2. Is it important to make a definite decision to give up war and violence? Why or why not?

NOTES

1. J. Krishnamurti, *The First and Last Freedom* (San Francisco: HarperCollins, 1975), 185.

2. www.brainyquote.com/quotes/quotes/a/alberteins385842.html.

10

The Power of Dialogue

An enemy is one whose story we have not heard.
—Gene Knudsen-Hoffman

 How can dialogue contribute to building a world beyond war? Conversations that engage individuals in depth, conversations that are a living demonstration of the core practices of goodwill and no blame, have the potential to change the world.

For fifteen years, Len and Libby Traubman, an ordinary American couple, have sponsored gatherings in California homes where Jews, Palestinian Christians, and Muslims are given the opportunity to break bread together and share their stories. From this simple communal experience, these citizens have created a model for understanding that has been replicated not only in many living rooms but also in schools, colleges, and diverse religious institutions around the world.

Curious to see if the Soviet Union was really the "evil empire" they had heard it was, Len, a pediatric dentist, and Libby, a clinical social worker, visited that nation in 1984. Their positive experiences convinced the Traubmans that Russians were not the enemy but a "smart, beautiful and cultured people." Back in the United States, the couple devoted themselves to building American-Soviet relationships through dialogue. When the Cold War ended, they took the lessons they had learned and applied them to the Israeli-Palestinian conflict. "We realized that almost no Jews and almost no Palestinians here in North America or the Middle East have had an in-depth sustained relationship," Len Traubman explains.

"These are two peoples who don't know each other. There is a huge disconnect."

They began the Jewish-Palestinian Living Room Dialogue out of their San Mateo, California, home in July 1992, and recently held their 200th meeting. While they acknowledge that conditions in the United States make it easier for Palestinians, Jews, and Israelis to meet freely if they choose, they say their personal progress shows that dialogue can help bring about a similar understanding on a larger scale, in the Middle East itself.

As evidence of the value of their dialogue process, Len Traubman points out that fifteen years after holding that first Jewish-Palestinian conversations in their California living room, similar discussions are being held on a regular basis in more than sixty homes across the United States and Canada. In one of the conversations,

> A Palestinian man points out, "We own property there. Still have all the deeds to the property and at one point I hope I can exercise those deeds and I could live with Israelis in my homeland." A Holocaust refugee responds, "My family was kicked out of their homes, too, and they can't get them back. My family from Poland and from Russia, they can't get their houses back. They lived there for many, many generations and they're not getting their stuff back." The Palestinian persists, "What's wrong with sharing one acre out of the 50 you took from me? That's all I want."
>
> Palestinian-American Adel Nazzal was born in Ramallah in 1948, the year Israel became a state. Having grown up in refugee camps, witnessing the horror of war firsthand, Nazzal has devoted his life to peace. He says he joined the dialogue because political leaders have failed and this grassroots movement represents the best path towards peace.

"This group, I think, helps in the fact that it humanizes the other side," he explains. "There's a lot of misconceptions, people come in with an awful lot of baggage. Jews or Israelis have bad images of Palestinians; Palestinians have bad images of Israelis and a group like this, especially when we meet in each others' houses, share each others' food, we share a lot of trips together, I think that humanizes the other side, makes them more human."[1]

WHAT IS DIALOGUE?

Dialogue is exceptional communication that includes a quality of deep listening, with the intent to learn and expand one's frame of reference and worldview. Successful dialogue results in unprecedented new levels of compassion and creativity, and the breaking down of fear and stereotyping.

Dialogue is not ordinary conversation, which is often superficial and safe. It is not discussion, a word that shares roots with "percussion" and "concussion," ping-ponging ideas back and forth, waiting for what one wants to say next. And it surely is not debate, with winners and losers.

A prevalent feature of twenty-first-century media culture is the influential style of radio and television commentary that emphasizes the heat of disagreement for the sake of entertainment, not even rising to the level of civil discourse. People shout at one another or engage in extended monologues or serial interruptions. As this polarizing model spreads across the airwaves, it not only oversimplifies the national conversation about complex issues but also eliminates the very possibility of a search for solutions based on mutual respect for opposing views.

Dialogue is not conflict resolution. Rather, it is a foundational skill for entering into successful negotiation. It provides a medium to practice a deep shift of attitude: wanting the best not only for oneself but also for the "other." This comes from hearing—without "yes, but"—the personal narrative of another person, and discovering a humanity equal to one's own.

Maintaining goodwill, rejecting violence, resolving conflict, getting beyond "us and them," building agreement—all require the skills of dialogue. In dialogue we can engage the other with an open mind, knowing that people who can put listening ahead of their need to communicate their own point of view have a special power to transform relationships.

BEYOND ARGUMENT

The default setting of people is to take sides. People often aim to convince others to change their thinking by logically sound—but one-sided—arguments. Yet argument, no matter how persuasively presented, often completely denies the narrative or worldview of the adversary and results only in counterargument, closed minds, and ill will. We leave such encounters with a feeling of mutual frustration, sensing how much easier it is to generate heat than light.

Beyond argument and intellectual logic, successful deliberation and conflict resolution are nurtured by building relationships on the basis of respect and trust. The one who first listens to learn—with openness—is the one who has a far better chance of opening the mind of the other. This element of effective dialogue, even in a personal conflict, is one of the core experiences of living beyond war.

BEYOND IMPATIENCE

We live in a culture where we expect almost everything to happen instantly. But change takes time. People seldom instantly embrace a new idea or a new relationship. Rushing and pushing to "win" only makes the process take *more* time in the long run. The fastest way to make progress in getting people to think about new ideas is to slow down, build relationships, be certain everyone feels heard and respected, and enjoy the process.

Real power lies in being the first to listen with genuine curiosity, particularly if the person we are listening to is still in debate mode and not aware of our own effort to shift the conversation to dialogue. By listening until the person is completely finished, empty, and thoroughly heard, we are modeling the respect that we hope to receive for our own viewpoint, if and when the time is right to communicate it. Fulfilling this condition of effective communication often allows the participants the unexpected discovery of a mutual learning that neither could have realized alone.

The dynamic between ourselves and the people with whom we are trying to converse can be changed by our own receptivity. The more they disagree with us, the more we need to listen; the less talking we should be doing. Brenda Ueland shares her thoughts about the powerful possibilities of listening:

I want to write about what a great and powerful thing listening is. And how we don't listen to our children, or those we love. And least of all—which is so important too—to those we do not love. But we should. Because listening is a magnetic and strange thing, a creative force.

. . . This is the reason: When we are listened to, it creates us, makes us unfold and expand. Ideas actually begin to grow within us and come to life. You know if a person laughs at your jokes you become funnier and funnier, and if he does not, every tiny little joke in you weakens up and dies. Well, that is the principle of it. It makes people happy and free when they are listened to. And if you are a good listener, it is the secret . . . of comforting people, of doing them good.

. . . We should all know this: that listening, not talking, is the gifted and great role, and the imaginative role . . . And so try listening. Listen to your wife, your husband, your father, your mother, your children, your friends; to those who love you and to those who don't, to those who bore you, to your enemies. It will work a small miracle. And perhaps a great one.[2]

BEYOND INAUTHENTICITY

As listeners, we have an equal responsibility to express our own narratives and how we experience our life and our truth. In authentic dialogue, we respectfully and kindly ask our partners in conversation to please hear us, in equal response to our prior listening.

We can even temporarily leave the conversation altogether if we have to, admitting that we are becoming overwhelmed. It's acceptable to pause and ask for a time out until we are calmer. If we feel ourselves becoming upset by what we are hearing, we can describe our emotions, expressing them without blaming. "I feel deeply sad and devastated when innocent men, women, and children die in this war. I want people everywhere to learn to resolve conflict so that children don't have to see their families die around them."

Real listening cannot be merely a tactic. It becomes authentic only if we are genuinely curious, really taking in the other's story, point of view, and insights. Listening does not mean we agree, but only that we temporarily "suspend" our own frame of reference in order to be totally open. Ultimately, deep listening is one of the great acts of love and of healing.

When our own internal state is in good condition, we will be resourceful and capable of good communication in response to others. This requires noticing in detail how we feel inside while listening. Do we feel patient, free from fear, free of harsh judgment, respectful, compassionate, curious? These are learned skills, especially when we find ourselves in the midst of disagreement.

BEYOND FEAR: THE POWER OF STORY

A story is the shortest distance between people.

—Pat Speight[3]

Fear and mistrust of the "other" often encourages a reversion to the more primitive part of the brain, the amygdala, which leaves us with the limited alternatives of fleeing, fighting, or freezing. When the amygdala takes over, the more conscious and creative parts of consciousness can diminish in power. Talking with people who hold a different view can easily become war in miniature. As we both feel tensions rise, hostility can flash subtly from eyes to eyes, hearts beat faster, muscles stiffen. We feel uncomfortable and vulnerable losing the debate, the argument, the mini-war. We either rationalize that "might makes right," bulldozing our adversary, or we run away and avoid controversy altogether, becoming paralyzed and passive.

The power to overcome fear lies in connecting on the basis of our shared, equal humanity. Conversations go in more creative directions when people have heard one another's personal stories and life experiences. When we have understood on a deep level where people are coming from, it often changes the conversation significantly. Some want to lock up drunk drivers and throw away the key because they lost a child in an accident caused by alcohol abuse; others support the Iraq war because they have a daughter on duty there. We begin to walk in one another's shoes.

The life-changing, world-changing attitude shift that dialogue offers is this: we begin to want the best not only for ourselves but also for the other, equally. After such a shift, any process of conflict resolution moves more easily to successful completion.

BEYOND DRIFT

Because the reptilian parts of our brain can take over in stressful moments, it is essential to decide in advance to reject violence. A simple yet compelling example is the decision not to spank children. The decision itself can help parents discover creative, effective alternatives to violence, including the violence of disregarding or devaluing a child's point of view.

In this context, the more aware we are of our own childhood conditioning, the better we can respond during conflict. Everyone has had negative, sometimes even frightening experiences with authority figures—including being ignored, or dismissed, or spanked—when young and vulnerable. In reaction, we often adopt those same authoritarian ways, and we can respond negatively to people who seem to us to hold rigid or dictatorial attitudes.

By understanding that we may relive past experiences and consciously deciding in advance to reject violence, we can choose dialogue instead, be the listener, and transform confrontation into effective communication.

BEYOND ASSUMPTIONS

Our conditioning and limited life experience often leads us to perpetuate dangerous, incorrect assumptions about people. Entering a conversation assuming we know another's mind-set and motives can become a self-fulfilling prophecy that increases disagreement. Dialogue begins with a spirit of charity and an open exploration of the other as a human being like oneself. Then we can avoid ascribing bad motives. People who hold different views do so with a genuine sense that they are principled, good, correctly motivated, and right. From the other side, they may seem rigid or fearful or unaware, just as to them we may seem unrealistic, self-righteous, idealistic, disloyal, naïve, or weak. Both stereotypes can be overcome through clear communication over time.

BEYOND BOXES

What good am I if I'm like all the rest
If I just turn away, when I see how you're dressed
If I shut myself off so I can't hear you cry
What good am I?

—Bob Dylan[4]

To understand our world and know how to respond to it, we tend to organize our life experience into boxes of interpretation and meaning. We do the same with people. For convenience, we give each other labels—conservatives, liberals, and progressives; doves and hawks; Democrats, Republicans, Libertarians; Muslims, Christians, Buddhists, Jews, Reform Jews, Shia or Sunni Muslims, atheists; young, elderly. This helps us to respond as best we can and to survive. If we label people, sometimes we feel we don't need to communicate authentically with them or even consider them. This is not dialogue, and it denies the value of diversity. Excluding people moves them toward hopelessness, desperate acts, and ultimately war itself.

These boxes also cheat us out of experiencing relationships. Categorizing can cause us to feel separate. And labels are totally inadequate to encompass the full dimensions of our fallible uniqueness. They completely miss the depth of human beings and their hunger for more profound communication and reconciliation.

When I meet a man, I am not concerned about his opinions. I am concerned about the man.

—Martin Buber[5]

BUILDING A SHARED VISION

Many emerging models of successful communication and conflict transformation and resolution on the world scene are taking place outside the halls of government. Citizens who refuse to be enemies and insist on engaging on a mutual level have created these models. This is the "citizens' century," according to Dr. Harold Saunders, the U.S. diplomat who helped fashion five successful Arab-Israeli treaties. Saunders named citizen initiatives the "public peace process" and urged an expanded process of dialogue at the 1991 Beyond War conference for Israeli and Palestinian citizen leaders.

In this new "citizens' century," the old, uncreative discussions and debates between parties who insist that they are right and wish to dominate the "other" are giving way to the much more effective and workable process of dialogue. As the Muslim Sufi mystic Rumi wrote, "Out beyond rightdoing and wrongdoing there is a field. I'll meet you there."

Saunders asserts that "peace" treaties often fail to take hold permanently because governments and peoples will not proceed down a road if they cannot see what is around the corner. The open-ended process of dialogue helps in discovering not only the other person, culture, or nation but also new paths into the future together. "What's your vision of how terrorism might come to an end?" "What is your vision of a real Middle East community?" Well-chosen questions can help reframe a conversation and take a relationship to a more creative level.

Global Mindshift,[6] a grassroots organization that promotes in-depth conversations on the Internet, developed ten significant questions to promote thoughtful dialogue:

- How can we best prepare our children for the future?
- What does sustainability look like to you? How do we get there?
- How do humans need to adapt to survive the changes predicted for this century?

- How do we shift from "me" to "we" on both the local and global levels?
- How can we, as Gandhi said, be the change that we want to see in the world?
- What kind of economic structures can best support a shift to sustainable living?
- How should we re-invent the political process so that people feel that they have a voice?
- What kind of leadership does the world need now?
- How can we balance our personal needs with the most pressing needs of our community and the larger world?
- What can we do to reduce or eliminate violence in the world?

Such broad questions, posed in a spirit of genuine curiosity and goodwill, can lead to meaningful and open-ended conversations that enable real changes in thinking. It is also a useful exercise to think of effective questions to ask candidates for public office:

- In the light of all the costs of war, and given the fact that our country seems to get involved in a war every decade or so, what can people, community leaders, and elected officials do, and what can the government of the United States do, to prevent wars from happening?
- What criteria should determine how to slow and finally stop the proliferation of nuclear weapons and materials, as well as guide nuclear nations in their attempts to reduce their stockpiles?
- What model should the United States be for the world for nonviolent conflict resolution, humanitarian aid, support for international law, and collaboration with other countries?
- What changes are needed in the current structure of the United Nations to make it a more effective vehicle for peace and order in the world?

- Unilateral preemptive war may have opened a Pandora's Box. How can we, with the rest of humanity, back away from this troubling precedent?
- How do international arms sales affect the economy, stability, and prospects for order in the developed and developing world?
- Many people in the Arab world blame the United States for the plight of the Palestinians, with whom they identify. How best can the United States help the Israelis and Palestinians achieve agreement on coexistence?

The force which threatens to blow the world asunder resides not in the clouds or mountains but in the invisible heart of the atom. The inner force too, which like the power of the atom can either remake or shatter civilization, resides in the smallest unit of society, the individual. The individual is the secret advance base from which the power sets out to invade committee rooms, mothers' meetings, county councils, parliaments, continents and nations.

—Laurens Van Der Post[7]

QUESTIONS FOR DIALOGUE

1. Think of a time when you really felt someone was listening to you. How did it make you feel? When someone was not listening? What was the feeling?
2. What has been your experience of argument and debate? Of dialogue? How would you describe the difference?
3. What questions come to mind that would lead to a constructive dialogue about what our country and its relationships should stand for on the level of principle?
4. What does it mean to "reframe" an issue so that all parties in a dialogue have an opportunity to gain a new understanding of it?

5. If you had the opportunity to ask questions of candidates for national public office, what would you ask?

NOTES

1. Excerpt from an NPR broadcast with Jan Sluizer; see http://traubman.igc.org.

2. Brenda Ueland, "The Art of Listening"; http://traubman.igc.org/listenof.htm.

3. http://traubman.igc.org/story.htm.

4. Bob Dylan, "What Good Am I?," from *Oh Mercy*, Columbia Records, 1989.

5. www.nl.edu/academics/cas/ace/resources/martinbuber.cfm.

6. http://global-mindshift.org.

7. Laurens Van Der Post, *The Dark Eye in Africa* (New York: William Morrow, 1955), 115.

11

Hope

If the dynamics of the universe from the beginning shaped the course of the heavens, lighted the sun, and formed the Earth, if this same dynamism brought forth the continents and seas and atmosphere, if it awakened life in the primordial cell and then brought into being the unnumbered variety of living beings, and finally brought us into being and guided us safely through the turbulent centuries, there is reason to believe that this same guiding process is precisely what has awakened us in our present understanding of ourselves and our relation to this stupendous process. Sensitized to such guidance from the very structure and functioning of the universe, we can have confidence in the future that awaits the human venture.

—Thomas Berry[1]

 In one tiny corner of our galaxy, the universe has invested in a high-risk experiment: you and me. We are beings powerful enough to foul and possibly destroy our own life-support system, but we also possess the capacity for self-conscious reflection, wonder, and growth. We can learn to see ourselves in each other in spite of our duality, our apparent separateness. We can see the outlines of our common fate beyond our conflicts. We can work together in a fuller awareness of our interdependence. Will we rise to this immense challenge?

Far from being impossible, the possibility of moving beyond war is inherent in the fact that we humans are creatures of successful change. During the four billion years of life on this planet, not one of our biological ancestors made a fatal mistake before reproducing. To survive for that length of time in a constantly changing environment, our ancestors had to be masters of change.

With the advent of human consciousness, the ability to change expanded into the mental dimension. Using our minds, we accumulated knowledge and experience that we passed down through generations. Civilizations flowered. We developed cultural and religious traditions, and created magnificent beauty— architecture, music, and dance. We explored the outermost and innermost reaches of existence and gained sophisticated understanding of the laws that govern the universe.

We applied these laws to develop ever more advanced and powerful tools—communications, transportation, medicine. We moved mountains, changed riverbeds, harnessed the power of water, wind, oil, and sun. We explored ocean depths and outer space. We eradicated diseases. We put men on the moon and brought them safely back to Earth. We explored the far reaches of the solar system. With our technological resources, we have become the dominant source of change on planet Earth.

The ability of our ancestors to adapt successfully to constant changes in the environment lives in us today, creating tremendous potential. Our capacity to destroy virtually all life on this planet constitutes an unprecedented environmental change. Never before have we been handed an ultimatum of this magnitude.

On the positive side, never before have we been handed an *opportunity* of this magnitude. At almost the same time that scientists and engineers gave us the nuclear ultimatum, they also provided us with the means to eliminate hunger, overpopulation, and other occasions for war. They gave us inexpensive mass communication that can reach into every corner of the globe to share diverse insights into our common fate. They gave us satellites and seismic detectors that can verify compliance with test-ban treaties; they gave us insights into the mischievous workings of our own psyches; and they gave us the ability to travel around the world and meet with one another on a person-to-person basis.

The history of our species is a record not just of the dreary repetition of war and killing but also of the emergence of outcomes too surprising to have been foreseen. Technologically, humans have shifted from being hunter-gatherers, to farmers, to builders of suspension bridges. Politically, we have moved from the absolute rule of kings to representative government to the knowledge that international protocols of law and conflict resolution are essential to our survival.

As these changes have taken place, the gift of unexpected positive outcomes from unpromising situations has been the rule, not the exception. The historian Howard Zinn writes,

> What leaps out from the history of the last hundred years is its utter unpredictability. This confounds us, because we are talking about exactly the period when human beings became so ingenious technologically that they could plan and predict the exact time of someone landing on the moon, or walk down the street talking to someone halfway around the Earth.
>
> The end of World War II left two superpowers with their respective spheres of influence and control, vying for military and political power. The United States and the Soviet Union soon each had enough thermonuclear bombs to devastate the Earth several times over. The international scene was dominated by their rivalry, and it was supposed that all affairs, in every nation, were affected by their looming presence.
>
> Yet the most striking fact about these superpowers was that, despite their size, their wealth, their overwhelming accumulation of nuclear weapons, they were unable to control events, even in those parts of the world considered to be their respective spheres of influence.
>
> . . . Apparent power has, again and again, proved vulnerable to human qualities less measurable than bombs and dollars: moral fervor, determination, unity, organiza-

tion, sacrifice, wit, ingenuity, courage, patience—whether by blacks in Alabama, peasants in El Salvador, Nicaragua and Vietnam, or workers and intellectuals in Poland, Hungary, and the Soviet Union itself . . .

Political power, however formidable, is more fragile than we think. (Note how nervous are those who hold it.)[2]

Surprise also comes in the form of leaders with real vision and a genuine desire to use political power for the common good. Who could have anticipated the remarkable entrance upon the world scene of Mikhail Gorbachev? Martin Hellman, a professor of electrical engineering at Stanford who worked with his Soviet counterparts in the scientific community to assemble a book of essays about the dangers of accidental nuclear war, writes,

I think part of the problem is that major changes don't seem as big in hindsight . . .

In the same way, I think that looking back at ending slavery or women getting the vote loses much of its impact in terms of convincing people that humans are capable of radical change. Rather than seeing the miracle of the change that did occur, people seem to focus on the evil of those who supported the status quo of the time. Instead of "Look what miracles humans are capable of!" the attitude becomes more of "Look how bad human beings can be!" *The problem is that people are viewing the change from the wrong side in time.* [emphasis added]

Back in the 80's when people used to ask me, incredulously, how the change might occur that would end war, I told them, "Assuming we make it—and that is far from certain—and I had a crystal ball that told me how the change will occur, I wouldn't dare tell you. You'd lock me in the looney bin." All major changes seem to occur like that, seeming impossible up until they happen, after which they appear totally understandable and normal. If, for example, in 1800, I had told someone that slavery would end by white men dying in a civil war partly motivated so that black people could be free, what would have been the response? Or, to take a more recent example, how would people have reacted to a prediction, prior to Gorbachev's coming to power, that the Cold War would end when a Chairman of the Communist Party of the Soviet Union lifted censorship, encouraged free debate, and refused to use military force to prevent the disintegration of the Soviet Union? Open up that looney bin! Yet, today, people tend to lose sight of the miracle that was Gorbachev. Miracles seem to work like that, becoming invisible from frequent viewing.[3]

Let us recall also the near miracle of Reykjavik in October of 1986, when Mikhail Gorbachev and Ronald Reagan almost agreed to abolish all nuclear warheads in their two countries. They came as close to ending the possibility of nuclear war between those two superpowers as the administrations of Khrushchev and Kennedy came to inadvertently beginning it during the Cuban Missile Crisis.

If the nuclear powers built enough agreement among themselves, it would be even easier today to make the miracle of nuclear-weapons abolition a reality. Reciprocal reduction of these weapons to zero would proceed cooperatively, not unilaterally. This example would be a tremendous incentive to less-powerful countries to relax their attempts to possess such weapons as equalizers. If the superpowers dismantled their warheads, how different would be the quality of moral and diplomatic pressure the world community could exert on those who assume they need to join the nuclear elite. Success with abolition could lead to a more general relaxation of tensions, and a renewed focus of leaders and citizens on the enormous challenges of planetary sustainability.

Such mutual initiatives have a solid chance of becoming

mainstream thinking in the end because we can count on self-evident truth to motivate not only ourselves but also others from whom we may still feel alienated.[4] How many of our supposed adversaries may be longing for an opportunity to break out of the vicious circle of their fear of us, and ours of them? When we actively manifest our own goodwill, we bring out the goodwill in others.

In a world beyond war, the Golden Rule, that ancient expression of oneness, will flower into its finest form: the most creative initiative is that which strengthens both receiver and giver. In the parent-child or teacher-student relationship, the best in the giver is called forth by the need of the receiver to be nurtured or taught. The psychoanalyst Erik Erikson, in his 1964 essay "The Golden Rule in the Light of New Insight," extends this idea of mutual strengthening to the relations between nations:

> Nations today are by definition units of different stages of political, technological and economic transformation . . . Insofar as a nation thinks of itself as a collective individual, then, it may well learn to visualize its task as that of maintaining mutuality in international relations. For the only alternative to armed competition seems to be the effort *to activate in the historical partner what will strengthen him in his historical development even as it strengthens the actor in his own development—toward a common future identity.*[5]

By implication, Erikson goes to the heart of American exceptionalism. He critiques our sense that our unique good fortune and power allow us to assume that our ways are best—not only for ourselves, but for everyone else, too. Other nations often experience the power of the United States as, "Do as we say, not as we do." What if, instead, we were to base our foreign policy on activating in our adversaries what will strengthen them in their historical development even as this strengthens our own identity and development as a nation? Isn't this the ultimate definition of "win-win"?

Further, there is a dimension to what Erikson suggested that might not have occurred to him at the time he wrote in the mid-twentieth century: his sense of mutuality must be applied to the relationship between us humans and our threatened life-support system, to the symbiotic earth-human relationship. When we strengthen it, we strengthen ourselves. A further implication of the principle that all people on Earth are created equal is the sense that all living beings, the trees and the foxes and the bees, have an "equal" right to exist in viable habitats, not only because our own health ultimately depends on the health of the living earth that they fertilize and pollinate but also because they have a value in themselves as fellow beings of what Thomas Berry has called the "sacred community" of the Earth. This sense of connectivity with the whole system will become an essential context for the way people work together in the future. Ecological thinkers such as John and Nancy Jack Todd have begun to map out the design parameters of water and land restoration projects where the means truly are the ends in the making.[6]

Former Vice-President Al Gore has proposed, with characteristic visionary boldness, that the United States end its dependence on carbon-based fuels in one decade, while oilman T. Boone Pickens has advanced his own plan for capturing wind energy in the midwestern United States. The political will and the resources to implement such enormous projects will only be fully released when we decide on a vision of security that puts national and global sustainability ahead of an obsolete competition for military primacy. This release into taking care of the Earth is also, as Gore has repeatedly emphasized, a tremendous potential expansion of economic opportunity.

Together with the effort to meet our global environmental challenges, building a world beyond war is the great task of our historical moment. War is obsolete in the same way unbridled consumption of limited planetary resources is obsolete: our earthly home is too fragile and finite for the destructive power of either. To truly live beyond war, we must discover how to end our war with our life-support system. As Jonathan Schell said in a 2007 interview,

> Global warming, which is a whole new way of doing our-selves in, does create a radically new context . . . When I wrote *The Fate of the Earth,* back in 1982, I said that, first and foremost, nuclear weapons were an ecological danger. It wasn't that our species could be directly wiped out by nuclear war down to the last person. That would only happen through the destruction of the underpinnings of life, through nuclear winter, radiation, ozone loss. There has been an oddity of timing, because when the nuclear weapon was invented, people didn't even use the word "environment" or "ecosphere." The environmental move-ment was born later.
>
> So, in a certain sense, the greatest—or certainly the most urgent—ecological threat of them all was born before the context in which you could understand it. The present larger ecological crisis is that context. In other words, global warming and nuclear war are two different ways that humanity, having grown powerful through sci-ence, through production, through population growth, threatens to undo the natural underpinnings of human, and all other, life. In a certain way, I think we may be in a better position today, because of global warming, to grasp the real import of nuclear danger . . .
>
> In a sense, the nuclear dilemma is the easy crisis to solve. It does not require us to change our physical way of life; it just requires a different sort of political resolve. Technically, ridding the planet of such weapons is very feasible. We've already gotten rid of half the ones that existed at the peak of the Cold War. So, it's almost as if it's a preliminary item, something to get out of the way as we try to save the Earth from the other, newer ecological dangers that threaten our existence.[7]

Because the ecosystems of the Earth are so stressed, conflict on every level will only increase in the future. In order to sustain human life, a corresponding increase in our capacity to understand and resolve conflict nonviolently will be crucial. Moving beyond war will not usher in utopia. It will only free our energies and those of our children for challenges equally as demanding as fighting wars. We will need to make difficult choices about every functional aspect of our lives, from finding sustainable clean sources of energy to containing crime and disease to consolidating our food supply. But the three guiding principles provide a map to help us navigate through the shoals of these decisions. Starting from our common desire for a healthy planet, moving beyond "us and them," we can work our way back down to the resolution of more local conflicts, newly aware of how they nest in that larger context.

By expanding our foreign aid for projects that meet real human needs, we will increase our own security. We can cooperate on agreements based in international law, obedience to which is enlightened self-interest. Diplomacy undertaken with an attitude of goodwill widens the understanding of common interest among all parties, beginning a "virtuous circle" that is the active opposite of the vicious circle of war and terror. After the defeat of Germany and Japan in 1945, America saw that it was in its own interest to help those we had defeated become stable and prosperous. Now we need to think in terms of "Marshall Plans" that prevent war as well as ones that allow recovery after wars. Beyond "us and them," what makes "them" more secure makes "us" more secure.

As John Robbins asserted in chapter 1, the immense assets we presently devote to armaments and war will be more than enough to eliminate starvation and malnutrition, provide shelter and safe drinking water, restore our threatened ecosystems, foster democratic institutions, end illiteracy, and stabilize human population—worldwide. Even assuming a period of extended transition when internationally mandated peacekeeping forces would be needed to prevent conflicts from spiraling out of control, such initiatives would themselves constitute a major step beyond war between nations. War itself would be illegal, and large-scale conflicts would be resolved under a robust and internationally supported legal system.

The interrelated crises presently challenging us underline the sense that the human species has been stuck at what might be called an adolescent stage of development, characterized by obsession with an illusory independence and by rebellion against inevitable limits. We are being both pushed and invited to mature into a new stage, a stage of young adulthood, where we fall in love with the great work of nurturing the communal family not only of humans but also of all the forms of life—which brings us full circle, back to the words of Brian Swimme's eloquent foreword: "This work, whose side effect is to draw forth our noblest human qualities, will enable a new Earth Community to blossom forth, one as different from the twentieth-century Earth as a butterfly is from a cloud of hydrogen gas."

In whatever way we each contribute to building a world beyond war, we will be strengthening ourselves while at the same time giving the greatest gift we could possibly give to everyone on this small planet. This will above all be a special gift to children. In the kind of world we all want, adults will become the role models that children need, while children will flourish in an environment of security and hope that prepares them to be adults in their turn. To the extent that we hand over to them a safer world and give them the strengths to manage it, our children will put the three guiding principles and core practices to work in ways that we cannot even imagine.

I dream of giving birth to a child who will ask, "Mother, what was war?"

—Eve Merriam[8]

This era can be the best of times or the end of time, depending on which direction we humans take at this fork in our journey. To avoid extinction, we must take the path that leads to life. When we succeed in changing the way we think about war, we will not only arrest our drift toward catastrophe, we will flourish in ways we have only dreamed about. It may take longer than we hope, or it just might happen more quickly than we can imagine.

Even if the end of war does not come in our lifetimes, we know we can live beyond war in our own persons. The hope lies with you and me—and the meaningful work we must all share. We will not all respond in the same way, but if each of us, consistent with our talents and our energy, does something, together we *can* build a world beyond war.

We are the ones we've been waiting for.

—Elders of the Hopi nation

QUESTIONS FOR DIALOGUE

1. How does Erik Erikson's restatement of the Golden Rule differ from traditional formulations of the rule? How does this difference change the meaning of cooperation between nations? Of a mutual ecological relationship with the earth?
2. What is the relationship between ending the war between humans and the "war" of humans against natural systems?
3. Think about the events in your own life, positive and negative, that have brought about significant change. Imagine who you might be without these events.
4. What was new in this book? If anything was new, how has this changed your thinking?
5. Has this book made its case about the truth and practicality of the three guiding principles and the core practices that derive from

the principles? What are the strongest arguments you can come up with against that case?

6. Think about the well-known Hopi expression "We are the ones we've been waiting for" in terms of the content of this book. Knowing what you know now, how will it change what you do and how you do it?

NOTES

1. Thomas Berry, *Evening Thoughts*, ed. Mary Evelyn Tucker (San Francisco: HarperCollins, 2006), 169.

2. Howard Zinn, "The Optimism of Uncertainty," in *The Impossible Will Take a Little While*, ed. Paul Rogat Loeb (New York: Basic Books, 2004), 63-64.

3. Martin Hellman, unpublished reminiscence. Hellman, a professor of electrical engineering at Stanford University, was the coauthor with Anatoly Gromyko of Beyond War's joint project with Soviet scientists, *Breakthrough: Emerging New Thinking* (New York: Walker, 1988).

4. See excerpts from Njabulo Ndebele's commencement speech at Wesleyan University in appendix D, p. 172.

5. Erik Erikson, "The Golden Rule in the Light of New Insight," in *Insight and Responsibility* (New York: W. W. Norton, 1964), 242.

6. Nancy Jack Todd, *A Safe and Sustainable World: The Promise of Ecological Design* (Washington, DC: Island Press, 2005).

7. Interview with Schell, http://www.truthout.org/docs_2006/120507I.shtml.

8. thinkexist.com/quotation/i_dream_of_giving_birth_to_a_child_who_will_ask-/204524.html.

Appendixes

A. Further Reading and Viewing

DVDs

"Beyond War: A Roadmap for Citizens"
"A Force More Powerful"
"The Fog of War"
"In the Valley of Elah"
"Iraq in Fragments"
"No End in Sight"
"The Powers of the Universe" with Brian Swimme
"The Road to Guantanamo"
"Stop-Loss"
"Waging Peace"
"Why We Fight"

Books

Allison, Graham. *Nuclear Terrorism: The Ultimate Preventable Catastrophe.* New York: Times Books/Henry Hold, 2004.

Berry, Thomas. *Evening Thoughts: Reflecting on Earth as Sacred Community.* Edited by Mary Evelyn Tucker. San Francisco: HarperCollins, 2006.

Bohm, David. *On Dialogue.* Edited by Lee Nichol. New York: Routledge, 2000.

Campbell, Joseph. *The Hero with a Thousand Faces.* Third edition. Novato, CA: New World Library, 2008.

Doerken, Maurine. *One Bomb Away: Citizen Empowerment for Nuclear Awareness.* Los Angeles: A.W.O.L. Ink, 2002.

Egeland, Jan. *A Billion Lives: An Eyewitness Report from the Frontlines of Humanity.* New York: Simon & Schuster, 2008.

Erikson, Erik. "The Golden Rule in the Light of New Insight." In *Insight and Responsibility.* New York: W. W. Norton, 1964.

Esposito, John, and Dalia Mogahed. *Who Speaks for Islam: What a Billion Muslims Really Think.* New York: Gallup, 2008.

Ferencz, Benjamin. *Planethood: The Key to Your Future.* Coos Bay, OR: Love Live Books, 1991.

Fry, Douglas P. *Beyond War: The Human Potential for Peace.* New York: Oxford University Press, 2007.

Gromyko, Anatoly, and Martin Hellman. *Breakthrough: Emerging New Thinking.* New York: Walker, 1988.

Heard, Gerald. *Training for the Life of the Spirit.* Eugene, OR: Wipf & Stock, 2008 [original, London: Cassell, 1942].

Hersey, John. *Hiroshima.* New York: Knopf, 1985.

Johnson, Chalmers. *Blowback: The Costs and Consequences of American Empire.* Second edition. New York: Henry Holt, 2004.

Johnson, Robert. *Owning Your Own Shadow: Understanding the Dark Side of the Psyche.* San Francisco: HarperSanFrancisco, 1993.

Jones, Seth G., and Martin C. Libicki. *How Terrorist Groups End: Lessons for Countering Al Qa'ida.* Santa Monica, CA: Rand Corporation, 2008.

Judt, Tony. *Reappraisals: Reflections on the Forgotten Twentieth Century.* New York: Penguin, 2008.

Keen, Sam. *Faces of the Enemy: Reflections of the Hostile Imagination.* San Francisco: Harper & Row, 1991.

Kegan, Robert. *The Evolving Self: Problem and Process in Human Development.* Cambridge, MA: Harvard University Press, 1982.

Krishnamurti, Jiddu. *Freedom from the Known.* San Francisco: Harper & Row, 1975.

Kumar, Satish, and Freddie Whitefield, eds. *Visionaries of the 20th Century: A Resurgence Anthology.* Totnes, Devon, England: Green Books, 2006.

Kuriansky, Judy. *Beyond Bullets and Bombs: Grassroots Peacebuilding between Israelis and Palestinians.* Westport, CT: Praeger, 2008.

Lakoff, George. *Don't Think of an Elephant: Know Your Values and Frame the Debate.* White River Junction, VT: Chelsea Green, 2004.

Macy, Joanna. *Despair and Personal Power in the Nuclear Age.* Philadelphia: New Society, 1983.

McCarthy, Cormac. *The Road.* New York: Knopf, 2006.

164 • *Appendix A*

Moran, Terence P., and Eugene Secunda. *Selling War to America: From the Spanish American War to the Global War on Terror.* Westport, CT: Praeger, 2008.

Mortenson, Greg. *Three Cups of Tea: One Man's Mission to Fight Terrorism and Build Nations—One School at a Time.* New York: Viking, 2006.

Myers, Edward A., and Melissa Waterman. *Turnaround: Musings on the Earth's Future.* Gardiner, ME: Tillbury House, 2004.

Pape, Robert. *Dying to Win: The Strategic Logic of Suicide Terrorism.* New York: Random House, 2006.

Saunders, Harold. *Politics Is about Relationship: A Blueprint for the Citizens' Century.* New York: Palgrave Macmillan, 2005.

Schell, Jonathan. *The Fate of the Earth.* New York: Knopf, 2000.

———. *The Abolition.* New York: Knopf, 2000.

———. *The Unconquerable World: Power, Nonviolence, and the Will of the People.* New York: Metropolitan Books, 2004.

———. *The Seventh Decade: The New Shape of Nuclear Danger.* New York: Metropolitan Books, 2007.

Sharp, Gene. *Waging Nonviolent Struggle: 20th Century Practice and 21st Century Potential.* Boston: Extending Horizons Books, 2005.

Stone, Douglass, Bruce Patton, Sheila Heen, and Roger Fisher. *Difficult Conversations: How to Discuss What Matters Most.* New York: Viking, 2000.

Swimme, Brian. *The Universe Is a Green Dragon: A Cosmic Creation Story.* Santa Fe, NM: Bear, 1985.

———. *The Hidden Heart of the Cosmos: Humanity and the New Story.* Maryknoll, NY: Orbis Books, 1996.

Swimme, Brian, and Thomas Berry. *The Universe Story: From the Primordial Flaring Forth to the Ecozoic Era—A Celebration of the Unfolding of the Cosmos.* San Francisco: HarperSanFrancisco, 1992.

Todd, Nancy Jack. *A Safe and Sustainable World: The Promise of Ecological Design.* Washington, DC: Island Press, 2005.

Tolle, Eckhart. *A New Earth: Awakening to Your Life's Purpose.* New York: Dutton/Penguin, 2005.

Ury, William. *The Third Side: Why We Fight and How We Can Stop.* New York: Penguin, 2000.

Wallace, B. Alan. *Genuine Happiness: Meditation as the Path to Fulfillment.* Hoboken, NJ: John Wiley, 2005.

Weinberger, Sharon, and Nathan Hodge. *A Nuclear Family Vacation: Travels in the World of Atomic Weaponry.* New York: Bloomsbury USA, 2008.

Wilber, Ken. *A Brief History of Everything: The Eye of Spirit.* Boston: Shambhala, 2000.

Wink, Walter. *Jesus and Nonviolence: A Third Way.* Minneapolis: Fortress, 2003.

Web Sites

http://beyondwar.org (the official Web site of Beyond War)

http://traubman.igc.org (Len and Libby Traubman's initiatives to get Israelis and Palestinians to hear each other's stories)

http://global-mindshift.org (a Web site that connects people globally around the idea that to change the world you must change your mind)

http://www.combatantsforpeace.org/aboutus.asp?lng=eng (Web site for an organization that was formed by Israeli and Palestinian soldiers who work together to resolve conflict nonviolently)

http://ee.stanford.edu/~hellman/opinion/Resist_Not.html (Martin Hellman writes about Tolstoy's, and his own, encounter with resistance)

http://www.laonf.net/Default.aspx (reports on nonviolent initiatives within Iraq)

http://www.cnvc.org/org.htm (Marshall Rosenberg's Center for Nonviolent Communication)

http://www.psr.org (Physicians for Social Responsibility)

http://www.ippnw.org (International Physicians for the Prevention of Nuclear War)

http://www.fas.org (Federation of American Scientists—a reliable source for information on weapons of mass destruction)

http://www.thefriendshipforce.org (Friendship Force is an international organization that promotes goodwill and understanding through travel and exchange)

http://www.uri.org (United Religions Initiative is geared toward promoting dialogue among various faith traditions, promoting better
understanding and reducing us vs. them thinking)

http://www.masteringthepowerofnow.com/ (Ken Wilber talks about
Eckhart Tolle and spiritual practice)

http://www.nuclearsecurityproject.org (Kissinger/Nunn/Shultz/Perry
NGO to free the world of nuclear weapons, funded by Ted
Turner)

http://nuclearrisk.org (a Web site providing resources to those who wish
to assess and lower the risks associated with nuclear deterrence)

B. Excerpts from a 2002 Editorial
by Matthew Happold, Professor of Law,
University of Nottingham[1]

Is [the second Gulf War] war illegal without a second UN resolution?

The prohibition of the use of force is a foundational rule of international law. Only two exceptions are permitted: the use of force in self-
defence, or with the express authorisation of the UN Security Council
exercising its powers under chapter VII of the UN charter.

Iraq has not attacked the US, the UK or their allies, nor is there any
evidence that it is about to do so. Force may only be used in self-defence
in response to an actual or (according to some commentators) an immi-
nent armed attack. Therefore any arguments based on self-defence fail.
What the US national security strategy has advocated are pre-emptive
attacks on countries which may threaten the US. The use of armed force
in such circumstances is contrary to international law.

What about UN resolution 1441?

Security Council resolution 1441 does not authorise the use of force.
Any attack on Iraq would consequently be illegal.

Resolution 1441 finds Iraq to be in "material breach" of its disarmament obligations under earlier Security Council resolutions. It gives
Iraq a "final opportunity" to comply with its obligations and, to that
end, establishes an onerous and rigidly-timetabled programme of Iraqi
disclosures and UN inspections.

Failures by Iraq to comply are to be reported to the Security Council, which must then "convene immediately . . . to consider the situation and the need for full compliance." The resolution also recalls that the council has repeatedly warned Iraq of "serious consequences" as a result of its continued violations of its obligations.

But the resolution does not authorise the use of force. The term "serious consequences" is not UN code for enforcement action (the term used is "all necessary measures"). And, in their explanations of their votes adopting resolution 1441, council members were careful to say that the resolution did not provide such an authorisation.

Why, then, does the [British] government say there is a legal case for war?

It is difficult to know on exactly what grounds the government is basing its arguments that there is a legal basis for war, in the absence of a second Security Council resolution. Ministers have been less than explicit as to what that basis might be, and the government has refused to release the advice given them by the law officers and Foreign Office lawyers.

Nevertheless, there are arguments, if not very convincing ones, that the proposed US and UK action would be lawful. In particular, it is argued that Security Council resolution 678 (1990) provides express Security Council authorisation for force. That resolution, adopted by the Security Council in response to the Iraqi invasion and occupation of Kuwait, authorised the American-led coalition to use "all necessary means" to liberate Kuwait and restore peace and security to the region.

Hostilities in the Gulf War were then terminated by resolution 687 (1991), which imposed a lengthy list of obligations on Iraq, including several regarding disarmament. Iraq is in breach of those obligations. Indeed, resolution 1441 found it to be in "material breach" of them. Accordingly, so the argument goes, the authorisation to use force granted the US and the UK by resolution 678 has been re-activated.

However, there are problems with this analysis. First, it is generally considered that Security Council authorizations of force are only for limited and specific purposes. In the case of resolution 678, the authorisation to use force terminated with the adoption of resolution 687. Secondly, such an analysis was specifically rejected by Security Council members in their explanations for their votes on resolution 1441. The general view was that resolution 1441 did not provide for "automaticity," that is, it did not trigger any authorisation to use force.

Finally, it might be thought that even if resolution 678 did permit the USA and the UK to use force to enforce Iraq's disarmament obligations, it does not provide authority for regime change.

C. Excerpts from an Editorial in the *Wall Street Journal* by Henry Kissinger, Sam Nunn, George Shultz, and William Perry[2]

Nuclear weapons today present tremendous dangers, but also an historic opportunity. U.S. leadership will be required to take the world to the next stage—to a solid consensus for reversing reliance on nuclear weapons globally as a vital contribution to preventing their proliferation into potentially dangerous hands, and ultimately ending them as a threat to the world.

Nuclear weapons were essential to maintaining international security during the Cold War because they were a means of deterrence. The end of the Cold War made the doctrine of mutual Soviet-American deterrence obsolete. Deterrence continues to be a relevant consideration for many states with regard to threats from other states. But reliance on nuclear weapons for this purpose is becoming increasingly hazardous and decreasingly effective.

North Korea's recent nuclear test and Iran's refusal to stop its program to enrich uranium—potentially to weapons grade—highlight the fact that the world is now on the precipice of a new and dangerous nuclear era. Most alarmingly, the likelihood that non-state terrorists will get their hands on nuclear weaponry is increasing. In today's war waged on world order by terrorists, nuclear weapons are the ultimate means of mass devastation. And non-state terrorist groups with nuclear weapons are conceptually outside the bounds of a deterrent strategy and present difficult new security challenges.

Apart from the terrorist threat, unless urgent new actions are taken, the U.S. soon will be compelled to enter a new nuclear era that will be more precarious, psychologically disorienting, and economically even more costly than was Cold War deterrence. It is far from certain that we can successfully replicate the old Soviet-American "mutually assured destruction" with an increasing number of potential nuclear enemies worldwide without dramatically increasing the risk that nuclear weapons will be used. New nuclear states do not have the benefit of years of step-by-step safeguards put in effect during the Cold War to prevent nuclear accidents, misjudgments or unauthorized launches. The United States and the Soviet Union learned from mistakes that were less than fatal. Both countries were diligent to ensure that no nuclear weapon was used during the Cold War by design or by accident. Will new nuclear nations and the world be as fortunate in the next 50 years as we were during the Cold War? . . .

Ronald Reagan called for the abolishment of "all nuclear weapons," which he considered to be "totally irrational, totally inhumane, good for nothing but killing, possibly destructive of life on earth and civilization." Mikhail Gorbachev shared this vision, which had also been expressed by previous American presidents.

Although Reagan and Mr. Gorbachev failed at Reykjavik to achieve the goal of an agreement to get rid of all nuclear weapons, they did succeed in turning the arms race on its head. They initiated steps leading to significant reductions in deployed long- and intermediate-range nuclear forces, including the elimination of an entire class of threatening missiles.

What will it take to rekindle the vision shared by Reagan and Mr. Gorbachev? Can a world-wide consensus be forged that defines a series of practical steps leading to major reductions in the nuclear danger? There is an urgent need to address the challenge posed by these two questions.

The Non-Proliferation Treaty (NPT) envisioned the end of all nuclear weapons. It provides (a) that states that did not possess nuclear weapons as of 1967 agree not to obtain them, and (b) that states that do possess them agree to divest themselves of these weapons over time. Every president of both parties since Richard Nixon has reaffirmed these treaty obligations, but non-nuclear weapon states have grown increasingly skeptical of the sincerity of the nuclear powers.

Strong non-proliferation efforts are under way. The Cooperative

Threat Reduction program, the Global Threat Reduction Initiative, the Proliferation Security Initiative and the Additional Protocols are innovative approaches that provide powerful new tools for detecting activities that violate the NPT and endanger world security. They deserve full implementation. The negotiations on proliferation of nuclear weapons by North Korea and Iran, involving all the permanent members of the Security Council plus Germany and Japan, are crucially important. They must be energetically pursued.

But by themselves, none of these steps are adequate to the danger. Reagan and General Secretary Gorbachev aspired to accomplish more at their meeting in Reykjavik twenty years ago—the elimination of nuclear weapons altogether. Their vision shocked experts in the doctrine of nuclear deterrence, but galvanized the hopes of people around the world. The leaders of the two countries with the largest arsenals of nuclear weapons discussed the abolition of their most powerful weapons.

What should be done? Can the promise of the NPT and the possibilities envisioned at Reykjavik be brought to fruition? We believe that a major effort should be launched by the United States to produce a positive answer through concrete stages.

First and foremost is intensive work with leaders of the countries in possession of nuclear weapons to turn the goal of a world without nuclear weapons into a joint enterprise. Such a joint enterprise, by involving changes in the disposition of the states possessing nuclear weapons, would lend additional weight to efforts already under way to avoid the emergence of a nuclear-armed North Korea and Iran.

The program on which agreements should be sought would constitute a series of agreed and urgent steps that would lay the groundwork for a world free of the nuclear threat. Steps would include:

- Changing the Cold War posture of deployed nuclear weapons to increase warning time and thereby reduce the danger of an accidental or unauthorized use of a nuclear weapon.
- Continuing to reduce substantially the size of nuclear forces in all states that possess them.
- Eliminating short-range nuclear weapons designed to be forward-deployed.

- Initiating a bipartisan process with the Senate, including understandings to increase confidence and provide for periodic review, to achieve ratification of the Comprehensive Test Ban Treaty, taking advantage of recent technical advances, and working to secure ratification by other key states.
- Providing the highest possible standards of security for all stocks of weapons, weapons-usable plutonium, and highly enriched uranium everywhere in the world.
- Getting control of the uranium enrichment process, combined with the guarantee that uranium for nuclear power reactors could be obtained at a reasonable price, first from the Nuclear Suppliers Group and then from the International Atomic Energy Agency (IAEA) or other controlled international reserves. It will also be necessary to deal with proliferation issues presented by spent fuel from reactors producing electricity.
- Halting the production of fissile material for weapons globally; phasing out the use of highly enriched uranium in civil commerce and removing weapons-usable uranium from research facilities around the world and rendering the materials safe.
- Redoubling our efforts to resolve regional confrontations and conflicts that give rise to new nuclear powers.

Achieving the goal of a world free of nuclear weapons will also require effective measures to impede or counter any nuclear-related conduct that is potentially threatening to the security of any state or peoples.

Reassertion of the vision of a world free of nuclear weapons and practical measures toward achieving that goal would be, and would be perceived as, a bold initiative consistent with America's moral heritage. The effort could have a profoundly positive impact on the security of future generations. Without the bold vision, the actions will not be perceived as fair or urgent. Without the actions, the vision will not be perceived as realistic or possible.

D. A Voice from Africa: Excerpts from Njabulo Ndebele's Commencement Speech at Wesleyan University, May 2004

Njabulo Ndebele is a South African writer and professor who has held numerous academic positions, including vice chancellor of Cape Town University. He served for many years as the president of the Congress of South African Writers.

As I bring you greetings from South Africa, and specifically, from my community of scholars and students at the University of Cape Town, I also want to tell you that this year at our campus we celebrate the 175th year of our history. And you can see how far we have come as South Africa's oldest university.

By a remarkable coincidence, this is the same year in which our country celebrates ten years of democracy. While our country feels new, my university proudly feels somewhat old and hopefully wise and mellow. But we feel so intimidated by the passionate youthfulness of our country that we are doing everything we can to reinvent ourselves, and if we cannot succeed to actually look young, we may at least try to feel so.

I look at two hundred years of democracy in the United States, and wonder how you feel at this point. Do you feel old and hopefully wise and mellow? Or have you had more than two hundred years of passionate youthfulness? These are not the kind of questions to ask graduating students who, in the glory of their youthfulness, despite being young, are enjoying another birth today. Being old is far from their thoughts right now. Yet, I'd like to invite you to be old, not in age, but in the ability to stretch the imagination back into history for a brief moment, and I'll tell you why.

It's because I'm fascinated by what ten years of one country and more than two hundred years of another country means about what could possibly connect them.

Ten years ago my country achieved its freedom from tyranny and oppression. But we did not attain our freedom in the usual way. Our road toward liberty could be described as counterintuitive. This means that in a world that had become conditioned to think of conflict, particularly between black people and white people, as something that ends in victors and the vanquished, of the winner taking it all, it was strange first, not to have had a racial war, and secondly, it was strange that the contending races negotiated themselves out of conflict in favor of an outcome with two victors and no losers. Very strange! What kind of people give up power? And what kind of people give up the possibility of attaining it?

What most of us recognized in South Africa, at the very last moment, was just how much we needed one another. We realized that violent confrontation promised only destruction and a long life of shared misery. It was a choice we made. It was a choice against habit: the habit to seek to march into final battle. But there is something deeper about the choice of abandoning habit. It is something we have not reflected on fully in my country.

South Africans have been reflecting on the impact of the last ten years on their lives. Rightly, they have pointed to achievements that were beyond our imaginations. Within ten years, millions of people have their own houses, clean water, electricity, telephones, and universal early schooling. Major institutions of democracy such as parliament, the constitutional court, and other courts of law are used to resolve disagreement and conflict.

While these achievements are real and substantial, the deeper revolution in South Africa is not sufficiently appreciated. It is that we have not explored fully the implications of counterintuitive solutions.

I like to think of the matter this way: consider the white leaders who had been telling their followers by word and deed, and through the way they organized society into contrasts of black and white, power and powerlessness, wealth and poverty, division and wealth, that they had a divine right to be superior to other people, only for these leaders to declare almost overnight, that this view was wrong all along. How do you turn around in this way and retain credibility? Such leaders faced the fear of loss of credibility, the fear of being thought of having betrayed their people, of being thought of as having cowardly lost their nerve, and of having become weak at a crucial moment.

Many whites did feel betrayed. Many experienced confusion and a tremendous anguish, overnight. We remember one who in a fit of anger and frustration took his gun and shot at any black person he came across, killing many. Remarkably, many others of this kind recoiled in horror, before what they suddenly recognized in themselves.

On the other hand, consider the black leaders, symbolized by Nelson Mandela, who told their followers over decades of struggle that the white man understood only one thing: the language of violence. Freedom would come only at the barrel of a gun. Then one afternoon, on the very day that Nelson Mandela was released and tens of thousands of people waited for him to announce the beginning of a war, he told them, instead, about responsibility, reminding them about higher goals of freedom. How do you turn around this way and retain credibility?

What these events dramatized in an intriguing way was how two camps recognized mutual vulnerability through exposing themselves to considerable risk. In doing so, both sides resisted the attractive habit to be "tough." Being tough would have meant going to war at whatever the price. Each would have convinced themselves, truth was on their side. But thankfully, our leaders realized that being tough in this kind of way had caused much misery in human history. Caught in the clutches of danger, they discovered a new meaning of toughness as something much harder to do. They discovered that being tough was not so much about going to war, but about choosing to avoid it.

I believe there have been remarkable benefits from this that were profoundly human. South Africans gave up one-dimensional ways of thinking about one another. They gave up bias, stereotype, and preconception. In giving up historically determined certitudes, about themselves and one another, they sought to become far more tolerant, more open-minded, more accepting of personal or group faults. And that, for me, has been the greatest South African revolution: the transformation of deeply held personal and group attitudes and beliefs.

Perhaps to get a sense of just how far we have come let us recall what it was like living in South Africa just before we gave up war and violence as a solution to our problems. We remember how arrogant and self-righteous white society and the apartheid government were in those days, and how those attributes of behavior made them blind to their cruelty and the extent of it. They projected invincibility; as if things would be the way they wanted them to be to the end of time. The South African sun, they said, would never set. Being the most powerful military machine in South Africa, they had terrorized the entire subcontinent to submission. Their military capability had far outstripped their capacity to make it accountable to a higher moral order. The value of their humanity and their identity as a people became inseparable from, and even reducible to their weapons of war. They had become a manipulative state, obsessed with the mechanisms of its own survival.

They had the sense that they could stand up to the whole world, defy global opinion and do whatever they liked in the pursuit and promotion of their self-interest. In this they subjected their own citizens to the kind of constant brutality they meted out to others. In dealing with those they regarded as of lesser human quality than themselves, they were accountable to no higher morality. I remember that far from earning my respect, I deeply feared them. But it was a fear that went with much loathing.

It all seems like a bad dream now. Within a short space of time, the false sense of invincibility gave way to a deeply liberating sense of vulnerability, and even humility. That was one of the defining moments of our transformation: this embracing of uncertainty and vulnerability, which at the same time went the certitude that the past was unsustainable.

I have reflected much on this. What seemed to happen in this situation is that at the point at which you recognize mutual vulnerability between yourself and an adversary that won't go away, you signal a preparedness to recognize that there might be new grounds for a common humanity, whose promise lies in the real possibility that you may have to give up something of what has defined your reality handed down from a past that cannot entirely meet your best interests now and in the future. It is the humility that arises when you give up certitudes around what was previously the uncontested terrain of your value system and the unsustainable positions derived from it.

It is a delicate psychology that is at play here. Its full potential is possible only through a new discovered foundation of trust. It is about how to reconstitute identity, meaning, and credibility during that fragile moment when you and your adversary are both caught in danger of losing them all. It is about recognizing that both of you are caught in a situation of profound need for one another. But it is never easy to reach such a position, and if it can be so difficult for individuals, consider how difficult it must be for entire nations. Few are the moments in history when nations were in a position to accept that they could be wrong, that a value system that stood them so well through centuries may no longer be sustainable. In this, nations would rather go to war and be humiliated by unintended outcomes that showed them just how much they ignored an inner voice of caution, or that pride forced them to ignore it.

These reflections arise from my challenge to our graduation class, to stretch their imagination back into history to try to find out what could possibly connect a ten-year democracy with one that is more than two hundred years old. Well, what is this connection?

We still recall with excitement, in South Africa, the pains, traumas, and finally the pleasures of giving up a past. I believe that for you in the United States, the connection is your capacity to recall how exciting it was to do so, more than two hundred years ago. Where do you sense yourself to be at this juncture in this world that all of us live in? Is there reason to contemplate another birth? Is there need for some great leap to be taken? One of the greatest fears of political leadership is the fear of losing it. The question is: has the fear become so inordinate that it has become a real threat to the future?

So much has happened to you since 9/11 when the world was truly in solidarity with you. I wrote to my friends all over the United States, telling them how much I suffered with them. Since then I experience the world with increasing fear. I see the world becoming more and more divided. I sense that the situation we are in from a global perspective is not fundamentally different from where my country was ten years ago. I sense that the world needs a leading nation, or groups of nations, that can reassure, inspire hope, and offer fresh perspectives and new directions. I ask myself what nation or nations could possibly do that. I do not have an unambiguous answer. One moment I know it, the next moment I don't. Of one thing I am certain, though: the evolution of global awareness has led us to yearn for a world that needs to value highly multiple visions of itself. We need leadership to get us there. Where will it come from?

One thing is certain also: war and conquests in the twenty-first century suddenly look distressingly primitive as instruments for conducting the affairs of the world, no matter how advanced the weapons of war. We need a new value system for resolving world conflicts. In that value system the mechanisms for the resolution of conflicts and disputes would be founded on the principle that it is possible and even desirable to achieve mutually affirming solutions: to have mutually respectful victors and no losers. The value system based on the single predetermined solution, often one that is imposed by force of arms, will not result in mutually affirming outcomes, but can generate powerful human emotions that lead to perpetual global dissonance, anxiety, fear, and despair.

Now, I do have faith in the power of humanity to reinvent itself. In this, every graduation offers that possibility. That is why I am so happy for you, Class of 2004, who are moving out into the world, confident, that you will contribute to societal renewal through your infectious enthusiasm and zest for life . . .

NOTES

1. http://www.guardian.co.uk/world/2003/mar/13/qanda. politics.

2. *Wall Street Journal*, January 4, 2007.

Acknowledgments

Convention dictates that an author's name appear on the cover of a book. In the present case the nominal author has functioned more as an executive editor for the continuing clarification and updating of ideas and words that found their form through the work of many people. Behind this book lies the living history of a huge collective endeavor. In the 1960s Emilia Rathbun and her husband, Harry, a revered professor of law at Stanford, began an organization called Creative Initiative. This organization grew to a thousand people who spent twenty years becoming a highly educated and motivated community focused on human change. They did it through an intense study of scientific, spiritual, and philosophical wisdom. Out of this group emerged the collective attitude, motivation, and feeling of responsibility from which an audacious possibility could start.

This possibility emerged in the early 1980s as an international movement called Beyond War. Its initial impetus was the real fear that Cold War tensions between the superpowers could get out of hand and result in a nuclear holocaust. Using the film *The Last Epidemic,* produced by the Physicians for Social Responsibility, the Creative Initiative community evolved an educational curriculum that allowed them to dialogue effectively with citizens about the dangers of nuclear war. Fifteen couples took leaves from their professions and moved to other parts of the United States to engage with new people as full-time volunteers. By 1986, Beyond War had over 24,000 members active in twenty-three states and several other countries including Canada, West Germany, and the soon-to-be-dissolved Soviet Union. Its members hosted thousands of "Interest Evenings" and hundreds of "Orientation Meetings" in living rooms, churches, and synagogues. Through the work of Beyond War, citizens learned about the possibility of a life-extinguishing "nuclear winter," which could have resulted if even a small percentage of Soviet or American missiles had been launched—something that could still happen today. In an event the organization cosponsored with the International Physicians for the Prevention of Nuclear War in 1982, American astronomer Carl Sagan and Soviet physicist Sergei Kapitsa presented the concept of nuclear winter to more than eighty U.N. ambassadors. Not long after, a team of Beyond War members who were professional scientists, already in close communication with their counterparts in the Soviet Union, decided to collaborate on a set of papers exposing the extreme danger of a nuclear catastrophe and the parallel possibility of calming the antagonistic Cold War relationship. The result was the first book to be published simultaneously in the United States and the Soviet Union: *Breakthrough: Emerging New Thinking.*[1] At the same time, Beyond War was actively involved in the Contadora/Arias peace process in Central America, and also sponsored several international task forces that fostered multinational citizen diplomacy and facilitated cultural exchange.[2]

Each year from 1984 to 1989, Beyond War sponsored the Beyond War Award, given in recognition of the outstanding efforts of individuals or groups that modeled the nonviolent resolution of conflict. The award's nomination and selection process attracted international attention. Many distinguished figures, including Rosalynn Carter and Jonas Salk, served on the selection committee. The televised satellite "space-bridges" of the award ceremonies, one of which saw the first-ever real-time linkage of five continents by satellite, were viewed by millions of people worldwide who were able to experience the possibility of change through genuine connection across vast distances. In 1984, to give the award to the International Physicians for the Prevention of Nuclear War, large auditoriums in Moscow and San Francisco were each filled to capacity. The San Francisco Boys' Choir and the Moscow Boys' Choir sang together across the airwaves. As television cameras focused on the two participating audiences, separated not only by geographical distance but by all the alienation engendered by fifty years of Cold War, people in Moscow and San Francisco began to wave to one another. Many in both locations were moved to joyful tears.

At the end of the 1980s, in response to the optimism and relief many felt as the Cold War actually did come to an end, Beyond War broadened its mission and became the Foundation for Global Community. With the help of the foundation, after September 11, 2001, a group of concerned citizens in Oregon "re-launched" Beyond War as a discrete organization. One person deserves special mention in connection with this renewal, Gayle Landt, Beyond War's executive director from 2002 to 2007. Gayle gave her heart, soul, mind, and strength to ensuring the perpetuation of Beyond War. This book would not exist without her invaluable encouragement and guidance.

As Beyond War enters a new phase of growth, collaboration with Gayle and many others has here taken the form of a book whose purpose is to allow the further dissemination of its ideas for positive change. The author shepherded it to completion for the organization and donated it, along with any proceeds from its publication, to the organization and the movement at large. Literally hundreds of people have made editorial suggestions and provided enriching content. A heartfelt wave of thanks in the direction of all who helped, including close editors Bill Hallmark, Gayle Landt, and Nancy Tague, and contributors Len and Libby Traubman. The image of the mushroom cloud and tree is used courtesy of Jose Chicas, Avenging Angels, and Abolition 2000. Thanks also to our endlessly helpful editor and publisher, Robert Ellsberg, of Orbis Books. Finally, this book could not have been written without the support, encouragement, and example of Julia and Edward, Kenner, Chase, Joe Sr., Joe, Hillary, Anna—and Jean.

NOTES

1. Anatoly Gromyko and Martin Hellman, *Breakthrough: Emerging New Thinking* (New York: Walker, 1988).

2. See, e.g., http://traubman.igc.org.